HD
57.7
.G87
2008
RVS

W9-BXU-406

DATE DUE

FEB 08 2018

More Praise for *Leadership and the Sexes*

"*Leadership and the Sexes* is research-based and very reader-friendly, a Gender Development Kit that can be used by corporations to improve gender dynamics. Michael Gurian and Barbara Annis provide a scientific approach that breaks down traditional barriers and enables management to implement gender-based leadership rationally. This is an exciting book!"

—Dave Roth, former vice president of engineering, Packet Engines and Vivato Systems

"*Leadership and the Sexes* is a great book! Michael Gurian and Barbara Annis have captured the insights and science that explain so much about our gender differences. Their book is a priceless contribution to the business world as we learn how best to capitalize on the strengths of both sexes. It offers compelling scientific reasons for bringing us all to the table in equal, unique, and shared roles. I thank the authors for making sense out of a topic that others often cloud with political correctness. This book is right on target."

—Flip Flippen, president, the Flippen Group; bestselling author, *The Flip Side*

"*Leadership and the Sexes* is an important work and Michael Gurian and Barbara Annis are perfect to write it. Filled with practical, accessible information, this is a book that all of us need to read, whether we deal with men and women at work or (with those who lead) in our communities or families."

—Daniel Amen, M.D., neuropsychiatrist, the Amen Clinics; bestselling author, *Sex on the Brain*

"*Leadership and the Sexes* is one of the most comprehensive and powerful books ever written about how to harness the strengths, insights, and wisdom of women and men at work. A delightful, energetic, and important read, not only for this year, for this decade."

—Judith E. Glaser, CEO, Benchmark Communications, Inc.; author, *The DNA of Leadership*

"Much of what we have learned thus far about marketing to and leading men and women is based on observing cultural influences. *Leadership and the Sexes* brings a scientific basis that simply takes everyone's understanding to a whole new level. The opportunity this understanding brings to be more effective is a competitive advantage both in and outside our company."

—Jim Weber, president and CEO,
Brooks Sports

"*Leadership and the Sexes* is extremely valuable in two ways. Not only can everyone recognize something of themselves in it, but its numerous engaging examples of communication between women and men will help people interpret communication in the workplace more effectively. An additional bonus is that the authors provide the reader with recent research findings from neuroscience about brain differences between sexes, which may underlie some of the behavioral differences."

—Sandra F. Witelson, Ph.D., professor, Department of
Psychiatry and Behavioural Neurosciences,
Michael G. DeGroote School of Medicine;
Albert Einstein/Irving Zucker Chair in
Neuroscience, McMaster University

"This book offers such powerful insights into the daunting and often complex task of building gender intelligence inside an organization. I am sure it will be required reading for any business that is striving for a competitive advantage."

—Debbie McGrath, CEO, HR.Com

Leadership and the Sexes

Leadership and the Sexes

USING GENDER SCIENCE TO CREATE SUCCESS
IN BUSINESS

Michael Gurian
with Barbara Annis

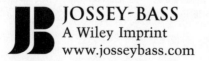

JOSSEY-BASS
A Wiley Imprint
www.josseybass.com

Published by Jossey-Bass
A Wiley Imprint
989 Market Street, San Francisco, CA 94103-1741—www.josseybass.com

Readers should be aware that Internet Web sites offered as citations and/or sources for further information may have changed or disappeared between the time this was written and when it is read. Readers should be aware that some of the anecdotes in this book, including some gathered from media reports, are composites of two or more comments or stories that needed to be shortened for narrative flow. In no cases have meanings been changed, and none involved statistics. Also, for collegiality and ease of reading, the authors have used "us" and "we" throughout the book to signify either or both of the authors.

Limit of Liability/Disclaimer of Warranty: While the publisher and author have used their best efforts in preparing this book, they make no representations or warranties with respect to the accuracy or completeness of the contents of this book and specifically disclaim any implied warranties of merchantability or fitness for a particular purpose. No warranty may be created or extended by sales representatives or written sales materials. The advice and strategies contained herein may not be suitable for your situation. You should consult with a professional where appropriate. Neither the publisher nor author shall be liable for any loss of profit or any other commercial damages, including but not limited to special, incidental, consequential, or other damages.

Jossey-Bass books and products are available through most bookstores. To contact Jossey-Bass directly call our Customer Care Department within the U.S. at 800-956-7739, outside the U.S. at 317-572-3986, or fax 317-572-4002.

Jossey-Bass also publishes its books in a variety of electronic formats. Some content that appears in print may not be available in electronic books.

Library of Congress Cataloging-in-Publication Data

Gurian, Michael.
    Leadership and the sexes : using gender science to create success in business /
Michael Gurian, Barbara Annis.
      p. cm.
    Includes bibliographical references and index.
    ISBN 978-0-7879-9703-8 (cloth)
    1. Leadership—Sex differences. 2. Management—Sex differences. I. Annis,
Barbara, 1954- II. Title.
    HD57.7.G87 2008
    658.4'092—dc22
                                                                        2008009376

Printed in the United States of America

FIRST EDITION

HB Printing   10 9 8 7 6 5 4 3 2 1

CONTENTS

PART ONE
THE THEORY: GENDER INTELLIGENCE—THE
NATURAL DIFFERENCES BETWEEN
MEN AND WOMEN
I

PART TWO

THE TOOLS: PUTTING GENDER
INTELLIGENCE TO WORK IMMEDIATELY
79

For my wife, Gail, and my daughters, Gabrielle and Davita
—Michael

For my husband, Paul, daughters, Lauren and Sasha, sons, Stephane and Christian, and stepsons, Zachary, Kelly, and Jeremy
—Barbara

Balance: state of equilibrium or equipoise; equal distribution of weight, amount, assets; an adjustment of accounts.

—AMERICAN COLLEGE DICTIONARY

ACKNOWLEDGMENTS

Like any product or business, a collaborative book of this kind is the work not only of its authors but also of many others who provide research, wisdom, and experience. No product happens without process, and no process without lots of help along the way.

Because this book grows mainly from material in the Gurian Institute's corporate gender training programs, it is crucial to begin by thanking Kathy Stevens, executive director of the Gurian Institute, for her organizational acumen; Pam Gomez Gil, a former manager at various major corporations—including Digital, Compaq, and Hewlett Packard—for her insights on women's leadership styles; and Katherine Coles, CEO of Mad Marketeer, and former VP of Marketing for Women in Technology International, who helped with research and development of the Gurian Institute training manuals. Many thanks also to Phil Gurian for his web help, Marcia Hilton and Don Stevens for their support, and Candice Fuhrman, who has shepherded this book through the publishing process.

These individuals are just a few of the thousands of men and women who have participated in the work of developing gender intelligence, and thus ensured that it makes a lasting difference in the lives of individuals and corporations all over the world. They, like us, could not succeed unless executives and corporations used this work and training in their corporations.

The following are just some of the executives and corporations we wish to thank for their confidence in gender work: Shahla Aly, Microsoft;

Jan Babiak, Ernst & Young; Subha Barry, Merrill Lynch; Clare Beckton, the U.S. federal government; Lynda Bowles, Mike Cook, Sean McConkey, Bev Simonson, and Yezdi Pavri, Deloitte & Touche; Charlie Coffey, RBC; Tony Comper, BMO; Maria Ferris, Susan Turner, and Bill Etherington (retired), IBM; Bob Haase, Theresa Fay-Bustillos, and John Anderson, Levi Strauss; John Hunkin, CIBC Wood Gundy; Chuck Ledsinger, Choice Hotels; Dennis Nally, Jennifer Allyn, Mary Beth Backoff, Kathy Nieland, and John Maxwell, PricewaterhouseCoopers; Mark Willis, Angela Anderson, Smith Barney Citigroup; Holly Taylor Sargent, Harvard University; and Bill Swanson, Raytheon.

The practical wisdom that emerges from the gender intelligence research in corporations, and the emerging teaching tools in this book, are immediately applicable to your team and workplace because corporations have field-tested gender innovations, with strong outcomes and success data. Among the trainers and associates who have facilitated gender intelligence work into corporations are Leslie Abdela, Lee Brower, Roxanne Cason, Dr. David Creelman, Judy Dahm, Judith Glasier, Peter Hagen, Christie Harwicke, Avril Henry, Lisa Hirsh, Philip Hoyt, Irene Hughes, Benedikte Jacobs, Mike Jay, Marty Kaplan, Akiyama Kenchiro, Dick Kimball, Mary Ellen Koroscil, George Labovitz, Stan Labovitz, Shannon Malolepszy, Tim Maroney, Marguerite McLeod, Dr. Keith Merron, Hubert Saint-Onge, Eiko Saito, Dr. Janet Smith, Bill Stevens, Julie Tereshchuk, Marion Tripp, Greg Van Asperen, and Jim Ward. Our thanks to you all for your hard work.

As you read this book, you'll note that it is science-based. Everything you read is connected to aspects of the human brain that have been researched by neuroscientists around the world. We profoundly thank the scientists who not only accomplish lab research in brain-based gender differences but also provide clinical advice and review. They help us remain at the leading edge of research and application. Particular thanks are due Ruben Gur, Ph.D.; Sandra Witelson, Ph.D.; Marianne Legato, M.D.; Helen Fisher, Ph.D.; Daniel Amen, M.D.; Linda Babcock, Ph.D., Lloyd Halpern, M.D.; Tracey Shors, Ph.D.; Judith Kleinfeld, Ph.D.; George Kohlrieser, Ph.D.; and Andrew Razhegi, Ph.D.

Finally, the authors wish to gratefully acknowledge the Jossey-Bass/ John Wiley publishing team. This group of women and men stands at the forefront of gender work. Rebecca Browning, Carolyn Carlstroem, Gayle Mak, Amy Packard, Susan Williams, Alan Rinzler, Byron Schneider, Mark Karmendy, Kristi Hein, Lori Ames, and many others are immensely creative people who know that if an idea can't be proven by practice in corporations themselves, it is generally worthless to business. We thank the whole publishing team for helping prove the ideas of this book in the corporate world and for helping us make these insights and tools public.

INTRODUCTION:
HOW GENDER INTELLIGENCE
LEADS TO BALANCED, AUTHENTIC LEADERSHIP

There are differences between men and women. . . . We can't ignore
a million years of history—at the office or in the living room.

—SHARON PATRICK, COFOUNDER AND FORMER CEO,

MARTHA STEWART LIVING OMNIMEDIA

THIS BOOK IS ABOUT THE PRACTICAL APPLICATION of information on male/
female brain differences in every aspect of your corporate life, from
workplace comfort to competitive edge to corporate bottom line. The
book helps you answer seven questions that we, Michael and Barbara,
have helped numerous leaders answer:

- Do I know enough about differences in men and women that are
  inherent in the human brain and thus will always be with us?
- Does my team understand the science of male/female brain
  difference to its maximum advantage?
- Is my company as a whole harnessing the innate and natural
  power of both male and female leaders?
- Is my company finding the right people for the specific jobs
  needed in the organization?

- Once we've acquired the skills of the right person, do we retain that person via a gender-intelligent corporate culture?
- Is my company set up to include enough gender mentoring structures, best practices for work/life and work/parenting balance, comfortable relations between women and men, and authentic leadership opportunities for both men and women?
- Has my corporation linked gender intelligence to its bottom line—that is, do we realize the financial rewards that increased gender intelligence can provide our corporation?

Michael and Barbara each came to these same questions from different countries of origin, different early corporate experiences, and different gender. When we brought our work together, we were immediately inspired by our commonality of vision.

Michael Gurian

Michael moved around a great deal as a boy; his father was a sociologist, his mother an anthropologist. Growing up in India and in various parts of the United States, Michael noticed two things that affected him profoundly later on: no matter where he lived, boys were boys and girls were girls; and no matter where he lived, boys and girls were different. While he was still a child, his insights into these phenomena could not go very deep, but they haunted him. His insights went beyond gender stereotyping, but until he learned about brain science, he could do no more than muse over personal experiences with both genders.

As he grew up, even before marrying, he felt pulled strongly into research and education that could help explain the phenomenon he saw—one that he was sure had a great deal to do with human nature. His initial work as a professional—university faculty member, family therapist, and corporate trainer—was built on research into natural sciences and brain science. He focused on using these sciences to build balance between women and men.

In 1983, when he was in graduate school, "gender roles" were discussed, but not male/female brain differences. Though the study of gender roles was and still is essential to human progress, it worried

Michael that few people asked, "What about actual gender; that is, can we talk about who we naturally are (biologically, chemically, neurologically) as males and females? And can we do it in a progressive way that would fully empower both women and men?"

In 1983, Michael set out on a journey, in tandem with a number of other researchers you'll meet in this book, to prove that the way to bring about true equality for women and men was not to avoid innate differences between women and men, but instead to use them to the maximum advantage of a corporation, community, school, and family. In the late 1980s, he began to develop a practical theory of male/female brain difference and a practical applications program.

A watershed moment in corporate culture came for Michael when he arrived at a Boeing facility to provide a gender training in the mid-1990s. His second daughter with his wife, Gail, had just been born; their first was three and a half. Michael walked through the doorway of the hangar-like building and looked up and into a huge airplane belly. The "vibe" in the Boeing facility was more "male" than female, with more men than women working the complex array of sheet metal, hydraulics, and circuitry. Women were being brought into this and other corporations quite quickly—the world had already changed quite a bit—and yet there were definitely fewer women than men in the facility, and there were also tensions, discomforts, lack of understanding between men and women in the training room.

Michael felt in himself the tension he had carried from childhood: between understanding that men and women were inherently different—neither one superior or inferior—and wanting to help make a corporate world in which that reality could translate into success for women, including his own daughters. Michael's job as a corporate trainer was to help resolve the tension by using information from brain science to facilitate success for both women and men. Would it work? Would both men and women appreciate the brain science and be able to apply it to their own workplace? Michael remembers being quite nervous about what would happen during his early years as a corporate trainer—the science was new, and initially many people reacted against it, insisting that who we are as women and men had nothing to do with nature but stemmed only from nurture.

However, when corporate trainees saw positron emission tomography (PET) scans of the male and female brain (you'll see brain scans in Chapter One of this book), their minds changed. In the following box is a snapshot of some of what we can see on brain scans.

??? Did You Know ???

A Snapshot of Gender Differences

It is important to note that brain differences between women and men exist all over the world, on all continents, in all cultures. The research in this book is gleaned from thirty cultures on all continents. The brain differences are thus universal, though their expression in a given country can be affected profoundly by cultural and environmental influences.

Businesses and leaders are now poised to deal with these sorts of differences because our neuroscience has developed new ways of understanding them. Neurobiologists have been able to track over one hundred biological differences between the male and female brain.

- There is 15 to 20 percent more blood flow in a woman's brain than in a man's at any given time. We will explore the affects of this difference on leadership throughout this book. Neither the male nor female brain is superior or inferior, but differences in blood flow in the brain enable different parts of the female brain to work simultaneously in ways that the male brain does not.
- The male brain shuts off (enters a rest state) many times per day, but the female brain does not shut down in the same way; as a result, women and men generally have different approaches to paying attention, completing a task, de-stressing/decompressing, "becoming bored," and even having basic conversations.

- The female brain processes information and experience to different parts of the brain at different times than does the male; the genders are equally intelligent, but intelligent in different ways. Thus we often see women and men focused on different things, ideas, outcomes, and even products.
- The male *hippocampus* (a major memory center in the brain) is generally less active than the female's during emotional and relational experiences in the workplace. There is also less linkage in the male brain between this memory center and the word centers of the brain, which is one reason men are less likely than women to talk about their emotional and relational experiences.
- The female *occipital and parietal lobes* are more active than the male's. This difference can affect, among other things, the negotiation of deals and daily conflict and communication situations, as we'll explain throughout this book. Men and women can both be great at negotiating, but they may get to the end result in significantly different ways.
- The male *temporal lobe* is generally less active than the female's, which means women have a greater comparative ability to hear words and to transfer what they hear, read, and see into written words. Men and women use words for different purposes at times—maximizing this difference can be essential to corporate success.

Since the early 1990s, everywhere Michael has shown the brain scans there has been general agreement that these tools and their applications for leaders can profoundly affect business. More recently, Michael showed these brain scans at a training at Cisco Systems, where participants found them fascinating. A lot has happened since the early 1980s and even the mid-1990s. Brain science has exploded in our culture, and the gender brain difference theory continues to develop all over the world. Michael, for his part, has become a teacher and consultant in male/female brain difference. A number of his books provide practical tools and philosophy based on male/female brain difference. Some—such as *What Could He Be Thinking?* and *The Wonder of Boys*—focus on helping people understand males, both boys growing up and adult males in relationships and at work. Others, such as *Leading Partners* and *The Wonder of Girls*, focus on helping people understand women and girls.

In 1996, Michael cofounded the Gurian Institute, a corporation that provides education in male/female brain difference in North America, Europe, Asia, and Australia. As Michael and his colleagues developed educational programs and materials in gender leadership for schools and communities, Michael searched for a woman partner in the corporate world with whom he could create a fully gender-balanced leadership book, based in brain science, for executive teams and corporations.

In 2002, Michael first spoke with Barbara Annis. Her journey as a woman and a gender expert resonated deeply with him. She was asking the same questions he was asking and provided gender leadership initiatives in many corporations Michael had not been to. As he got to know Barbara, Michael realized he had met an ally. Her insight has helped him continue developing the practical and strategic theory of male/female brain difference in a dynamically evolving leadership vision. Barbara's work has led her to years of experience, important success data, and powerful stories of genders working together.

Barbara Annis

Barbara also discovered the power of understanding the male and female brain from her own personal and professional journey. With her first job at Sony in the early 1980s, Barbara entered the business world focusing on how to fit into a male-dominant business environment. She worked and raised a family at the same time. Although wanting to be true to herself and her company, she soon learned she needed to become more like a man to succeed. She did quite well: she became Sony's first female sales manager. However, as she took on more and more male characteristics, she knew she was not being authentic to herself as a woman.

Seven years later, Barbara left Sony, taking her abilities and the company's investment with her. Barbara founded her own organization, Barbara Annis and Associates (BAAINC), which has twenty-seven associates and offices on four continents, determined to empower others to successfully develop authentic leadership as women and men.

A watershed moment came for Barbara during a panel discussion at a university law school audience. The audience was mainly young women lawyers; one of them asked a female senior partner at a Wall Street firm, "How did you as a woman get to where you are today?"

The answer came back quickly: "As a woman, you have to be ready to change yourself into someone you might not have thought you'd ever be." As the senior partner described her journey through this kind of change, detailing how every morning when she woke up she girded herself for the workplace that awaited her, the young women in the audience sat still, eyes wide. At a certain point, she paused and said, "Well, let me say this, if you asked my family to look at me when I'm working they would not recognize me. That's how different I become."

Barbara recalls feeling immense ambivalence as she listened to this fellow panel member. She honored what the woman had done and achieved, but the thought of the new young women sacrificing their authentic selves for their careers tore at her.

She said to her colleague, "That's the saddest thing I've ever heard." To the audience she said, "You can be part of a new evolution of gender relationships. You can be a woman and lead in your own way."

Barbara specializes in helping companies grow their competitive edge and bottom line through gender intelligence training and a science-based philosophy of gender balance in leadership. In 2004, she wrote *Same Words, Different Language,* which revealed some of the work she and her colleagues have done to help Deloitte & Touche, UBS Investment, Citigroup, IBM, PricewaterhouseCoopers, Xerox, Honeywell, General Motors, and many other corporations to maximize leadership potential through the gender and global leadership lens. As you'll learn in this book, these companies have saved and made millions of dollars by paying attention to the link between authentic leadership and gender intelligence.

A Gender Partnership

For Barbara, as for Michael, the evolution of how women and men work together is not just an exercise in organization and management; it is something that can touch the very core of our lives. It is also something to be done in partnership, as much as possible, between women and men.

This book brings together theory and applications developed over the last two decades by two practitioners committed to helping you become the most authentic leader possible. The book provides you with five leading-edge gender tools you can use both personally and in your executive team. These tools can help you build success in your corporation, no matter its size or service. By the time you finish this book, you should have tools in place that will help you accomplish the following:

1. You will increase your gender intelligence so that you can understand the men and women around you as you never have before. The brain science you will learn about in this book takes your work and relationships into the ever-growing world of neuro-leadership, which can be quite empowering. Our work in gender intelligence sits gratefully on the shoulders of such scientists as Jeffrey Schwartz of UCLA, such business gurus as Warren Bennis, and leading-edge companies like Cargill and AIG, all of whom have teamed up to explore neuro-economics, neuro-marketing, and the positive effect of understanding how the brain works in business. We and this book bring to this neuro-intelligence programming an added specialization in gender.

2. You will gain a feeling of authenticity as a leader, based on who you are as a man or woman. As you read this book, you will find help for putting into practice what you have learned, from such

thinkers and trainers as Bill George, Ken Blanchard, and Terry Pearce, about how to be an authentic leader. The work of authentic leadership asks questions such as "What role does leadership capacity play in driving organizational vitality?" "What specifically can leaders do to increase organizational performance?" and "What are the connections between leadership capacity, customer devotion, and employee passion?" Throughout this book, you'll find answers that benefit from the much-needed addition of a gender lens: "Who am I as an authentic female leader or male leader?"

3. You will see ways to supervise, negotiate with, and manage others (as well as design and market products) to increase your corporation's competitive edge, profits, and bottom line. If you have learned negotiation skills from the Eastern classic *The Art of War* or other sources, you'll see those principles expanded through the gender intelligence perspective of this book. If you've learned good communication skills from Pat Heim's work, or better management skills from Stephen Covey or Andrew Razeghi, you'll find those tools enhanced by adding the gender lens. The new gender work in this book erases nothing you've learned in the past—it adds new tools to your toolbox.

4. You will be better able to meet internal corporate goals for balanced leadership between women and men. If you and your leadership team are concerned with retention and advancement of women, you may have looked at the work of feminist economists such as Sylvia Ann Hewlett, of Columbia University. She and many others are exploring ways to empower female leaders. Indeed, there is a great deal of media and professional attention these days on the possible reasons that women have difficulties advancing in some corporations. This book, by providing a brain-based perspective and then focusing on proven solutions, provides answers you can use immediately. We are grateful to the corporations we've worked with who have been retaining and advancing more women, and gaining gender balance: their CEOs share innovations, data, and results with you in this book.

5. You will be better able to help your company and our fast-moving global economy to revise male/female relationships for the new millennium. As you deepen your understanding of women and men in this book, you will not only explore useful brain science, authentic leadership, and practical tools, but also participate in a new vision of "gender evolution." Gender is natural and it is evolving. In this book, you won't just focus on women—you'll also focus on men (a focus that is often lacking in contemporary books and materials on gender balance).

These five goals are inherent in every page of this book. We hope you'll take on these goals both as an individual reader and in your leadership teams. The gender differences this book explores go back, through human brain development, about one million years. Each of us has deep personal feelings about them. Open dialogue is crucial to beginning the journey of exploring who we are.

When we brought our assets together in this book, we did so because we, our respective colleagues, and the corporations we work with share a common vision. We are pushing for a corporate revision of both traditionalist and feminist notions of women and men—a revision that is already leading to a new era of gender relations. As you read this book, we hope you will enjoy moving your corporate culture forward in an immensely positive way, proven to be profitable for both women and men.

Science-Based Leadership

Rajeev Singh, president and CEO of Concur Technologies, a Seattle-based software developer, told us, "The scientific approach to gender and the PET scan tools not only are revolutionary, but hit people where they live. Until leaders see the PET scans and then see the science in action, we don't realize how this information can positively change business."

In Part One of this book, we'll lead you through this exciting and very applicable world of positron emission tomography (PET), magnetic resonance imaging (MRI), and single photon emission computed tomography (SPECT) scans—these tools are revolutionizing how we understand men and women. You'll get to know yourself and everyone you work with through the science-based lens, in every aspect of your corporate life. You'll see yourself reflected in numerous real-life examples of men and women leading and working—both in conflict or tension and also cohesively together.

In Part Two, you'll acquire and put to use our specific GenderTools for integrating gender understanding and your newfound knowledge. From running better meetings to negotiating better contracts, you'll gain skills for maximizing not only your own talents, but also those of your coworkers and teammates. You'll be poised to increase your company's overall success as you go into meetings, negotiations, conflicts, marketing, and sales efforts with women and men.

In Part Three, you'll take that exciting knowledge of male and female nature into an evaluation of how your corporation is doing in leadership and other areas impacted by gender. You'll look at key areas of balanced leadership between genders that you can act on immediately—questions and models for deploying and retaining much-needed female and male talent. You'll see the financial fruition of the hard work—how paying attention to gender at work leads to positive financial and human capital gains both for corporations as a whole and for your personal success. Specific case studies appear in Part Three.

Corporations that have been positively affected in many areas by this kind of gender work include IBM, Boeing, Microsoft, Proctor & Gamble, Unilever Corporation, PricewaterhouseCoopers, Royal Bank, BMO Financial, Deloitte & Touche, Levi Strauss, Nissan, Citigroup, Xerox, Ernst & Young—and the list goes on. Throughout this book, you'll meet executives from many of these corporations who have gained gender intelligence tools and worked at the forefront of the new gender evolution.

Gender Evolution

Between us, we and our spouses have nine children who are, like everyone in business today, coexisting as males and females in a corporate world that searches for new truths regarding women and men. All of us are now at a point of gender evolution that will impact not only the workplace, but also relationships, homes, schools, and society for a long time to come. The workforce today is more multigenerational than ever before. It is composed of men and women who are not only similar, but also different from one another. Each brings a unique male or female nature to the daily work.

As authors and trainers, we have not only observed corporations we work with, but also observed our children, and we feel strongly that each individual in leadership and the workplace today wants to be authentic in individual ways, yet also in partnership with diverse individuals. Workplaces are inherently competitive. People don't want special treatment—they want to prove themselves. Young women entering the workforce today know they must prove themselves to each other and to men. Young men entering the workforce today know that human workplaces are highly relational—they know they must engage relationally in ways their grandfathers did not have to do.

As you enjoy your workplaces, and as the young people you know move into the business world, we join you as authors and leaders in caring about both the present and the future, with an eye to what did and didn't work in the past. As you involve yourself in our GenderTools and gender intelligence insights, we hope you'll join us in using a science-based approach to gender, and enjoying this book as an adventure in male-female relations. It is a science-based adventure, and it may challenge you philosophically and practically; it is also written from a deep passion to help corporations grow and succeed, one woman and one man at a time.

Leadership and the Sexes

PART

The Theory

Gender Intelligence–The Natural Differences Between Men and Women

The workplace is a second home for most executives, managers, and employees, providing financial security, emotional connection, self-esteem, and at a very deep level, much of our sense of meaning and purpose. Into this workplace walk not only "people," but women and men. A business can't maximize its productivity, profit, and outreach unless it understands, from top to bottom, what makes males and females tick.

—PAM GOMEZ GIL, FORMER DIRECTOR, PROGRAM MANAGEMENT
AND QUALITY CONTROL, HEWLETT PACKARD

Understanding the Science of Gender

> Human evolution has created two different types of brains (male and female) designed for equally intelligent behavior.
>
> —RICHARD HAIER, PROFESSOR OF PSYCHOLOGY, UC IRVINE

IT CAN BE DIFFICULT TODAY TO TALK COMPLETELY AND HONESTLY about how men and women feel at work. Respectful humor is often helpful.

A number of years ago, a story began to circulate on the Internet. Some people thought it began with Stephen R. Covey, though no one knows for sure. It is a fictional transmission between a U.S. Navy aircraft carrier and Canadian authorities that provides us in the gender world with a humorous metaphor for beginning a dialogue. We get a special chuckle from this story because Barbara is Canadian and Michael is American—but the story could involve any countries and any cultures.

CND: Please divert your course 15 degrees to the south to avoid collision.

USA: Recommend you divert your course 15 degrees to avoid collision.

CND: Negative. You divert *your* course 15 degrees to avoid collision.

USA: This is the captain of a U.S. Navy ship. *Change your course now or countermeasures will be taken to ensure the safety of this ship.*

CND: This is a lighthouse. It's your call.

A lighthouse and a ship—they both have something essential to offer. At first, neither one understands what the other one is. Once they understand, perspectives change.

Is the lighthouse one gender and the ship another? No. For our purposes, the lighthouse represents human nature (*gender*), and the moving ship represents cultural shifts in use of gender (*gender roles*). In the science-based paradigm, gender comprises the male/female characteristics we are born with and the context in which we receive our early nurturing; gender roles are the roles that our society and we ourselves decide we should fulfill as women and men.

In this model, the lighthouse is "hard-wired"—it's been there a long time. The ship can't deny the lighthouse exists, nor change the "course" of the lighthouse—and, perhaps most important, it *needs* the light shining from the lighthouse to help chart its safe course. Though the ship initially feels threatened by the presence of the lighthouse (not knowing what it is), once it learns the character and value of this other presence, it can in fact navigate more safely.

The moving ship is the "soft-wired," changing part of the gender equation. The ship represents the gender roles we each bring to the workplace. These can change from generation to generation and from person to person.

When the ship doesn't have all the information the lighthouse possesses, our sense of gender roles, as individuals and a society, will often limit either women or men, increase gender stereotypes, misrepresent who we are as individuals, and lead to confusion, fear, and, ultimately, anger and anguish. When, however, the ship acquires crucial information about human nature—gender—it realizes the lighthouse is there, and it can more safely and more effectively navigate gender roles, gender issues, executive team development and trust, individual and personal concerns between women and men, and the whole workplace culture.

??? Did You Know ???

Gender Experiments Surprise Even the Experts

In the 1990s, the Canadian Broadcasting Corporation (CBC) created a short film that recorded an experiment in leadership styles between women and men. CBC didn't tell the participants the objective of the work they would do that day; the director simply divided the male and female leaders into two teams, and gave those team leaders the same instructions: build an adventure camp. The teams were set up in a somewhat militaristic style at first, including team members wearing uniforms, but also with the caveat in place that the teams could alter their style and method as they wished, as long as they met the outcome in time.

Leader one immediately created a rank-and-file hierarchy and gave orders, even going so far as to assert authority by challenging members on whether they had polished their shoes.

Leader two did not have the "troops" line up and be inspected, but instead met with the other team members in a circle, asking, "How are we doing? Are we ready?" "Anything else we should do?" "Do you think they'll test us on whether we've polished our shoes?" Instead of giving orders, leader two was touching team members on the arm to reassure them.

As part of the program, CBC arranged for corporate commentators to watch the teams prepare. Initially, the commentators (mostly men) were not impressed by the leadership style of leader two; the second team wasn't under control, members weren't lined up, and they lacked order (or so it seemed). The commentators predicted that team two would not successfully complete the task. Yet when the project was completed, team two had built an impressive adventure camp, as good as team one's, with some aspects that were judged even better.

When debriefing their observations, the commentators noticed that when team one was building the structures for their camp, there had been discord regarding who stood in charge and who had completed which job and who hadn't. Team one showed a lack of communication during the process of completion that created problems (for example, "Wasn't someone else supposed to do this?").

Team two, on the other hand, took longer to do certain things, but because of its emphasis on communication and collaboration during the building and enactment of the task (such as "Let's try this" and "What do you think about that?"), the team met the goal of building the adventure camp in its own positive way, and on time.

Which leader do you think was a man, and which one a woman? You probably saw the answer coming—the woman was leader two. The commentators who watched this experiment certainly knew about authentic leadership, different management styles, and the idea of diversity. But they weren't quite ready for the female leader to succeed so completely with her "nonmale" leadership style. They were—as many organizations' succession planning committees can be—unconsciously (and consciously) thinking the woman "just doesn't act like a leader," "just doesn't have things under control," "won't meet deadline," "is run by her staff." The committee may know she gets results, and it may even have her name on a short list, but the members can't quite get their heads around the fact that a woman's authentic leadership style doesn't need to look like a man's authentic leadership style.

The CBC experiment is just one ray of light coming from the lighthouse. The light being sent out into the world from experiments like this illuminates the differences between the male and female brain at work, especially in leadership roles. Although of course anything can happen in a social experiment that is being filmed—and in all the gender-related science we explore in this book, you'll be able to think of "exceptions to the rule" (you'll learn, in fact, about women and men who are actually hard-wired toward the middle of the gender/brain spectrum—that is, they have higher-than-average amounts of the other gender's brain characteristics)—at the same time, wherever you travel in the world, you will find that female leaders often share certain traits that are different from male leaders. Let's explore the biology of this difference, for it crosses all cultures, and it is fascinating!

Getting to Know the Gender/Brain Spectrum

The human brain is hard-wired (genetically coded with) its gender. As *gender* is not one thing or type, but very diverse, you will find throughout this book that your brain's male/female coding fits somewhere on a wide *gender/brain spectrum*. To start very practically discovering where your particular brain fits on the spectrum, go to the Appendix and fill out the gender/brain spectrum survey. We have developed this as a personal tool, usable by anyone. You can also go to the website www.bbc.co.uk/science/humanbody/sex/add_user.shtml and take the BBC's "What Sex Is Your Brain?" test. It is very detailed and accessible. If you have time, you may enjoy doing both.

Tools of Science: How the Female and Male Brain Are Studied

Beginning in the 1970s, researchers began to use medical technologies and computers to study gender in the brain. There are three techniques most used:

- *A PET scan* uses positron emission tomography to identify areas of neural activity. Scientists can locate the regions that become active while a person speaks, works, relates, loves, performs tasks. By comparing these "brain pictures" to those taken before or after a task, scientists gain insights about brain organization. PET scans from all over the world show that male and female brains are organized differently.
- *MRI scan* uses magnets to detect signals from particles with a positive electronic charge that act like compass needles in the magnetic field. Because the amount of oxygen found in blood affects its magnetic properties, MRI detects regions with changes in levels of blood oxygenation due to activity-related changes in blood flow. MRI can provide both anatomical and functional information for each subject, helping researchers accurately determine which brain regions are active in each task. MRI studies have shown that the regions of the male and female brain activate differently, no matter the subject's culture or continent of origin.

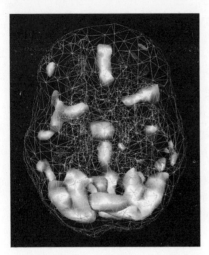 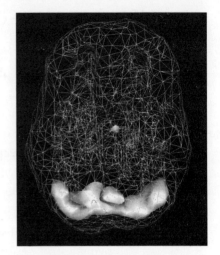

Figure 1.1. *Female at Rest.*   **Figure 1.2.** *Male at Rest.*

Source: Brain scans courtesy of Dr. Daniel Amen. Used by permission

- *SPECT imaging,* similar to PET and MRI, uses single photon
  emission computed tomography to provide lower-resolution
  images; it is much less expensive than PET. As you can see in the
  SPECT scans in Figures 1.1 and 1.2, the male and female brain
  look quite different in terms of brain activity. (These SPECT
  scans appear courtesy of one of the Gurian Institute's scientific advisors, Daniel Amen, M.D. He and his team at the Amen
  Clinics have done thirty-eight thousand brain scans.)

Equal but Different Intelligence

As brain science becomes more sophisticated, the results of studies
consistently indicate that although men and women produce equivalent intellectual performance, their brains do it differently.

We are different in the following ways:

- *How and what we remember.* Women take in more through each of
  their five senses than men do, on average, and store more of this
  material in the brain for later use. Thus they tend to remember
  more details during a conversation, for instance.

- *How we process words (and how many and what kind we use).* Women use more words than men. This includes reading and writing, not just speaking; that is, a man and a woman may speak the same amount of words in a week, but will not generally read and write the same amount.
- *How we experience the world.* New studies are indicating that even the cells in our retina may well be different, with female retinas tending to have more P ganglion cells (which see color and fine detail), and male retinas tending toward more M ganglion cells, which more easily see physical motion of objects moving in space around them.
- *What we buy and why we buy it. Because of these sensory differences,* women's buying is often more linked to immediate complex sensory experience than men's; for example, women more readily enjoy walking through a store and touching and feeling objects, while men will get less pleasure from this. Men, on the other hand, link more of their buying to both spatial enjoyment (such as video games, which are all about objects moving around in virtual space) and to performance competition and aggression identification. Thus we find more men interested in buying memorabilia from sports teams with which they passionately identify.
- *The way our midbrain (limbic system) and emotional processing works.* The approach to developing self-esteem and emotional intelligence can be quite different in women and men, especially because women's brains tend to link more of the emotional activity that is going on in the middle of the brain (the limbic system) with thoughts and words in the top of the brain (the cerebral cortex). Thus a man might need many hours to process a major emotion-laden experience, whereas a woman may be able to process it quite quickly. This often creates a lot of tension between women and men.
- *The amounts of white matter and gray matter in the brain.* Women have more white matter and men have more gray matter related to cognitive functioning in the brain. White matter connects brain centers in the neural network, whereas gray matter tends to localize

brain activity into a single active brain center. The white/gray matter difference is one reason the genders bring different perspectives to the same problem or design. Women tend often to be able to make crucial connections between widely disparate elements that men don't make; simultaneously, men tend to task-focus on one element or pattern without distraction better than women do.

How Does the Brain Get Hard-Wired for Gender Differences?

Each of us is a woman or man at a certain place on a gender/brain spectrum. Michael, for instance, might have more gray matter than his brother has, as well as more than Barbara has; Barbara might have more white matter than her sister or another woman, and so on. Although all women will tend to have more white matter and all men more gray matter, within these gender characteristics there is variety—that is the gender/brain spectrum.

How do the gender characteristics along this spectrum get wired into us individually? The answer can be best understood as a three-stage process. Where you fit as a particular woman or man on the broad gender/brain spectrum depends, in large part, on these elements:

1. On every X and Y chromosome are genetic markers for fetal development of female and male in the body and brain. You have your own genetic markers, coming from your parents and their genetic lines. This first stage of wiring occurred in you at your conception, when the particular X and/or Y chromosomes were passed to you.

2. The second stage occurs while a fetus is gestating in utero—your chromosome markers alerted your mother's body, and then your own fetal system, to produce hormonal surges from within testes or ovaries that helped your male or female body and brain grow.

3. After a child is born, genetic personality, temperament, needs, and gender traits signal who we are to parents and caregivers. As you grew, your body and brain continually guided your maleness and

femaleness, while the society and family nurtured various aspects of each (of course, during this time parents and society may have actually missed aspects of who you were, or tried to change who you were—even gender stereotyping who you were).

By the time you arrived at your first workplace, your gender was genetically, hormonally, neurally, and socially wired. It was and is a natural part of you.

Can the Brain Be Reprogrammed for Gender?

When we share this hard-wiring information in our workshops, someone inevitably asks, "But isn't the brain plastic and changeable?" They are asking, "But I thought gender was socially developed, not inborn, so we should be able to get women and men to be androgynous, right?"

If you've followed the current dialogue about brain science in the media these days, you've probably heard the term *plasticity*. That term is what the questions are about. "Anyone can learn to do anything." "Anyone can become anyone else." It can feel uncomfortable to say anything else, especially when talking about gender.

And so you might hear someone say, "Look, if you gave boys dolls every day for a year and you gave girls toy trucks every day for a year, wouldn't the 'plastic brain' finally change itself? The boy would become a kid who loves dolls and emotion-talk, and the girl would become a kid who loves construction sites and ninja video games."

In a recent training, a CEO asked the question this way: "If you talk to boys about their feelings every day for hours (and have them read and write about them), won't they end up becoming men who talk (and read and write about) feelings as much as women often do? Isn't the brain plastic, so these guys' brain centers would change to fit how they've been nurtured?"

This kind of question arises not only from our innate human curiosity but also from our personal and cultural fear that if we discover the human brain's gender characteristics to be hard-wired, this fact will keep boys from becoming emotionally healthy men and, perhaps most frightening, keep women from gaining equity in the workplace.

It is natural and socially very important for us to at first be suspicious of any kind of thinking that limits our opportunities based on sex and gender. We don't want to be restricted in abilities or self-expression! So we ask these questions.

As you may have yourself, we've asked these questions now for twenty-five years, in concert with male and female colleagues in the sciences and in corporations and communities. The brain-based answer is immensely liberating, for it includes both nature and nurture:

- First, gender in the brain is not as plastic as some other aspects of brain development—nor as plastic as the feminist movement theorized. Gender in the brain is, in part, chromosomally and neurally "locked in" in the same way that the genetic personality you are born with (extravert or introvert, sensing or perceiving, and so on) is, in part, chromosomally and neurally "who you are." Children who were born with male brains, for instance, but have had their genitals removed (in medically ordered procedures to solve specific medical problems) have still remained "male" in their thinking and being, in the same way that they remained extravert or introvert. Part of gender is hard-wired.
- Simultaneously, the genetic and nurtured expression of our genes—our DNA, then our neural formatting—is definitely and profoundly affected by the external environment. Every biological organism or mechanism exists in—and is shaped, to some extent—by its environment. Although the place we will inherently fit on the gender/brain spectrum is not as plastic as we once thought, the effectiveness of our functioning in a team with the other gender (and in marriage, family, and every aspect of life) can be affected profoundly by how gender intelligent our parents, society, and workplace become.

There is no either/or here, no nature versus nurture. That is ultimately what is most liberating about this brain-based/nurture-dependent point of view. Nature (who we are) is nurtured by environment (how we fit who we are into the environment we live and work in). Although genetics of gender preclude us from changing a boy into a girl or vice versa, environments affect the extent to which different genes get expressed and are viable—in this lies the heart of the opportunity debate in women's and men's lives. Equal opportunity must be given to each individual man and woman so that they, as differently but equally intelligent women and men, can discover how to nurture and express their own inborn nature in cohesive groups.

As you absorb this information and this thinking, you are standing at an evolutionary point in gender history. Whereas once a culture might well stereotype women and men when talking about difference, the new brain sciences can now move us forward to true partnership. Two hundred years ago—even thirty or forty years ago—nearly any information about women and men could be manipulated and skewed, as it was opinion, not science. Hypothetical scenarios about raising kids could be posited and debated, no matter how far-fetched. People came to believe that adult gender equality depended on erasing gender differences and making everyone the same.

Now, science is available, and corporations such as IBM, PricewaterhouseCoopers, Deloitte & Touche, Procter & Gamble, Unilever, and many others—that have paid attention to how inherently different the genders are—actually do *better* at advancing women's and men's success in the workplaces. Paying attention to who we really are makes it possible to create policies that satisfy our deepest needs as women and men, create partnerships based in mutual respect and support, and improve bottom lines through gender intelligence, gender balance, and evolving opportunities to become people of depth and vision.

For this to work, though, we all need to make sure we understand how much gender is tied up with our lighthouse genetics: this is the crux of gender intelligence. To move deeper into understanding the gender/brain information, and to move clearly into pushing beyond a nature-versus-nurture kind of thinking (to a nature-with-nurture approach), add *low plasticity* and *high plasticity* to your gender vocabulary. Leaders often find these terms intriguing, and a worthy distinction, one made by neuroscientists that we can understand and use immediately in our teams.

Personality (such as introvert/extravert) and gender (where you fit on the gender/brain spectrum) are aspects of who you are that have *low plasticity*. On the other hand, the language or languages you learn as a child involve brain functioning that is *highly plastic*. The languages you learn depend on what cultures you grow up in and move to (French in France, Japanese in Japan, English in the United States or UK, and so on).

Similarly, although *gender roles* can change based on your culture, your brain will still show up as male or female on PET, MRI, or SPECT scans, no matter where you go. So *gender* does not depend on where you grew up—the costume of how you manifest it will be affected by culture, but because it is something that has been developing over about a million years in our DNA, you'll see women in Saudi Arabia using more emotion-laden words than men, and women in the United States doing the same; you'll see women in North Africa remembering more sensory details than men, and women in America doing the same; you'll see men in all countries crying fewer tears, on average, than the women in those same countries.

Low plasticity does not mean there won't be cultural effects on your brain/gender genetics. For instance, you can certainly train boys to not cry and end up stifling their tears, and you can encourage boys to cry

??? Did You Know ???

Male and Female Tear Glands Are Different by Nature

Women throughout the world have higher levels of prolactin, which controls, among other things, the development of tear glands. Your gender base in prolactin levels will not change unless it is interfered with by a medication or chemicals; hence, generally, wherever you go (even in a culture that is friendly to male tears, like Italy) you see more tears falling from women's eyes than from men's. The chromosomal development of prolactin in the female body and brain and its resulting genetic expression in larger tear glands is just one aspect of female DNA that has low plasticity.

and girls not to and end up stifling girls' tears. But the changes won't change the children's brains from male to female and vice versa. That's the crux of what we've discovered scientifically in the last thirty years. Your individual genetics can include aspects that don't fit the male and female on your gender/brain spectrum analysis—you could be a man who cries a lot, for instance, or a woman who cries not at all—but when you look at yourself comprehensively from a gender lens, you'll most probably see that you are male or female.

What is the bottom line on all this? The brain is quite adaptable, but in areas of personality and gender it is also hard-wired. Even a boy brought up only by women or a girl brought up only by men will find that although he or she has been affected in certain ways through these life circumstances, he or she is still boy or girl, man or woman. One celebrity example of this that corporate audiences often find compelling is that of football players (or other athletic stars) like Bo Jackson, who talk in interviews about being brought up without significant men in their lives—that is, by a single mom and by other women—but who obviously have low plasticity of the male brain. Male athletes like Jackson who were nurtured mainly by women and ended up high-testosterone, high-muscle-mass, very spatial-kinesthetic, using fewer words than most women are very much male on the gender/brain spectrum.

As you move farther into this material, your internal frame as a leader (both a woman and a man) may well shift toward a next-stage and revolutionary understanding of gender and leadership. Along the way, we hope you'll find that discovering where *you* fit on the gender/brain spectrum feels like discovering a treasure: a liberating (albeit complex) part of who you are.

Burning Question: Are There Exceptions to the Gender Rules?

Having established that there is hard-wiring of male/female difference, it is crucial to not go forward without looking at exceptions to the rule. You may be one of these!

Ten years ago, Michael coined the term *bridge brain* to help people understand the exceptions: these include people whose brains share a number of characteristics of the other gender's brain, transgendered individuals, and people who just sense their brains may be toward the middle of the gender/brain spectrum. In Michael's corporate work especially, women would come up to him and say, "You know, I think I fit a lot of the qualities you're presenting as 'male brain.' I was a total tomboy as a kid; I couldn't sit still; I didn't like dolls much, which got me rejected by other girls; I was really good at physics but avoided reading for pleasure; I still prefer working alone to talking a lot with people; I'm not very emotional. . . ."

This woman is physically, emotionally, spiritually a woman, of course, and she isn't trying to limit or stereotype herself one way or the other; rather, she has always sensed instinctively that her brain doesn't quite work in the same way many other girls' or other women's brains work.

A similar thing happens for some men, as well. Recently a male CEO said to Michael, "You know, I want to say privately to you that all my life I've known I was a bridge brain, though I didn't have the language for it, and I certainly didn't know there were brain scans that could show it. But I was the kid who loved dolls and soft things, I didn't like team sports, I have always been more verbal and emotional than most guys. . . ."

This man pointed out characteristics in himself that show him to be higher in oxytocin and lower in testosterone (we'll talk more about this brain chemistry in the next chapter), with a brain formation that includes more "female" characteristics. Just as the bridge brain woman had humiliating and negative experiences as a girl for "not belonging," so too did this man as a boy for not fitting in with the guys.

What research into bridge brains is showing us scientifically is this: (1) every one of us has both our own gender's and the other gender's hormones and brain characteristics (hormones and the brain are "human," and we all share them); (2) yet if we are biologically male, we will tend toward being more male on the brain/chemistry spectrum, and if female, we'll tend toward female; and (3) some of us are closer to the other gender on the spectrum than others are. Some of us, in other words, are neurological "bridges" between genders.

You yourself might often see bridge brain women in the technology sector, just as you might see bridge brain men in the social services sector. The bridge brain women might be a lot like the woman who spoke to Michael, and the bridge brain men more likely than other men to multitask, care a lot about verbal and emotional material, and not be as competitive as other men or women around them.

Two scientists have especially helped us understand bridge brains in the last decade. They have been interested in how bridge brain activity shows up on brain scans. Both Daniel Amen, M.D. (www.amenclinics.com) and Simon Baron-Cohen, Ph.D. (New York, *The Essential Difference*) have been able to show how different a bridge brain woman's or man's scan looks from a more "male" or "female" scan. Baron-Cohen, for instance, has estimated that around one in seven men and one in five women are in the middle of the gender/brain spectrum.

It is much easier to see male bridge brains than female ones (because the male brain at rest shows up with so little activity, whereas the female's neural web shows up with more activity). If you compare Figure 1.3 to the scan of the male brain in Figure 1.2, you'll notice much more activity in the middle of the brain in this one—in the areas of emotional and verbal expression.

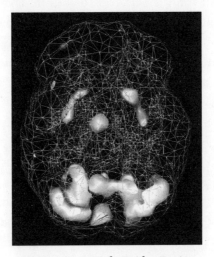

Figure 1.3. *Male Bridge Brain.*
Source: Daniel Amen, M.D.

For more understanding of bridge brain men, you might enjoy Michael's book *What Could He Be Thinking?* For more on bridge brain women, you might enjoy *The Female Brain* by Louann Brizendine. Especially if you are a bridge brain or if you work closely with one, you might find this kind of research very stimulating. It can feel like looking directly into the light coming from the lighthouse. In later chapters of this book, as we explore ways to retain more women at the highest executive levels, especially in companies that have been traditionally dominated by male brains, we will look again into the female bridge brain.

Before we leave the subject here, though, there is a twist in this research and thinking that Barbara began to notice about ten years ago. Some women would come up to her in a training and say, "I think I'm a bridge brain; I operate just like the male managers at work." But when Barbara asked, "Are you this way at home?" some of them paused and said, "No, not at all, just at work."

This answer can become part of the "lighthouse" we are working with in this book. It shows the immense adaptability of human beings to meet the perceived needs of their environments—these women have accessed parts of themselves needed to "become like men" so they could survive at work—but as we'll notice especially in Chapter Eight, when these women train themselves to counter their natural inclinations, they often push back, at some key point in their career, against having to give up "who they are." They end up leaving the workplace that invested immense resources in their development as leaders, but did not understand them as adult women.

Empowering Yourself and Your Corporation by Joining the Scientific Process

As we provide you with scientific information and scans showing various parts of the gender/brain spectrum, we hope you'll join with us and with scientists in using the science to help build your organization to its full power. All the work that each of us do to adapt scientific research for use in corporations would not be successful without the original laboratory work of the primary scientists studying gender in humans, animals, social history, and societies around the world. As you move into this world, through this book and its tools, it is important to note that the world of primary science does not operate in absolute agreement. Indeed, the science of gender is in constant flux. Increasingly, too, it is part of the public debate, whether in academics, in the media, or in your boardroom. Everyone has an opinion about the male and female brain!

This is where you can come in. As authors of this book, and as gender coaches and social theorists, we make sure to inform our strategies and ideas with scientific studies, and you'll see their application in this book. We hope you, too, will develop and pursue your own science-based opinions about gender. The process of building gender intelligence requires open debate and dialogue, grounded in scientific process.

To help you join this process, we've provided original studies throughout the Notes and Resources section of this book. They are fascinating, especially if you like reading scientific studies. They are also only the beginning of the journey toward gender intelligence. When we and our colleagues have interviewed a number of the scientists noted in this book—including Ruben Gur, Sandra Witelson, and Marianne Legato—we have found them to be enthusiastically at work on some new research design. They are constantly expanding the purview of gender science. We have also found them all to be in agreement on a warning: "Be careful how you use gender science." Stereotyping can destroy the effort to develop gender intelligence in human development. In the workplace, it can be counterproductive.

Join with Scientists in Analyzing Gender

Perhaps there is no more difficult line to walk in gender science than the "Avoid stereotyping" line. Where is the line? If you read just the popular media to get a sense of gender science, you can become very confused indeed! This happened recently when a headline popped up around the world, "Myth That Women Talk More

Than Men Debunked." It referred to a study of a small cadre of university students in Arizona, both male and female, who had been equipped with a device that counted the words spoken in a day. These young women and men spoke, on average, about the same number of words each day. The study's authors announced that, therefore, four decades of research on male/female brain difference was wrong—there is no verbal difference between women and men. If you do a web search on something like "gender and verbal skills," you'll find widespread reporting of this study (for instance, "Study: No Yap Gap," by Helen Kennedy, *New York Daily News*, July 6, 2007).

This study provides a crucial example of how we must all enter the scientific dialogue ourselves in order to see what is really happening with gender. It also shows how careful we must be in pursuit of gender science. It is not superficial stuff. It needs replication. It needs careful analysis.

The Arizona study, for instance, was very incomplete science. Analyzing it here can help create a template for your constant analysis—in your leadership team and in the rest of this book—of gender science.

- The study's authors implied that their study proved men and women use the same amount of words in a day; however, it measured only spoken words, not written and read words. In fact, women read and write more words per day, on average, than men, as has been proven by Ruben Gur and others (see, for instance, Halpern, Benbow, Geary, Gur, Hyde, and Gernsbacher, 2007).
- The study sample included just over two hundred people, all in one place. It did not replicate around the world, where there are around six billion women and men, boys and girls!
- The sample population consisted of university students at a university that relies heavily on verbal skills—this

pool of young people (both young women and young men) is already a more verbal pool than you would find in your neighborhood car mechanic's garage, or a city's construction site, or your own home, or even perhaps the corporation you are now leading.

As authors of this book, gender trainers, and a woman and a man who have each applied gender science for a quarter century, we come to our work knowing these caveats:

- There is no way to get complete agreement from everyone on what a scientific study regarding gender can mean for every individual. Scientists can disagree with one another, and they can disagree with the people who apply the science.

- If a basic idea or application of a piece of science isn't replicated, or carefully provided, or both, stereotyping and confusion can occur.

- Gender science is increasingly useful outside the university or academic laboratory, and thus a nonacademic population (of which you may be a part) is constantly weighing in on the science.

As we have helped corporations and communities apply principles of gender science, we've been able to gather information (what is called *wisdom of practice research*) from tens of thousands of people like you. When you read stories in this book or any of our other books about how corporations, individuals, schools, and family members have applied gender science, you are seeing a priceless kind of proof—corroborative, intuitive, and appearing worldwide.

Ultimately, we believe that for good gender science to be of use it now requires three major actors: the original scientists (many of whom appear in the Notes and Resources); the interpreters of the science for corporations and others (we, as theorists, trainers, and authors, fit in this category); and the leaders and others, like you, who apply gender principles every day, whether through training or through instinct. When you read this book and apply the science, we hope you'll hear all three voices represented, and we hope you'll listen to all three—especially your own voice, as a woman or a man.

The Lighthouse

For a few decades now, our corporate world has done a lot of wonderful things in the area of gender roles, but we are also stuck in many ways. We've avoided dealing with the lighthouse of gender biology—we've been afraid of it—and so we've been navigating without its light. In today's corporate world, power, leadership, control of assets—*all* are in flux, and economic pressures, globalization, media, the Internet are all affected by gender, even when we don't realize it. We need to be gender intelligent, even a little bit revolutionary! We need to move beyond both the traditionalist and feminist frameworks and look at the light that human nature itself is providing to all of us, now more than ever before: that light that can help guide every leader to the best possible outcome.

You've begun to look at the male and female brain through a biological lens. Can you see interesting applications not only to leadership at work, but also to home and family life? Everything we talk about regarding work has a mirror image in other male/female relationships.

In the next chapter, we'll increase the light and vision into daily manifestations of brain differences in *your* workplace—from self-motivation to management styles to communication styles. You'll be able to look more closely at how brain differences are utterly interwoven with your work and leadership, and you'll see fascinating applications elsewhere as well.

Note: To help you experience and absorb some of the brain differences and specific gender needs we'll show you in Parts One and Three of this book, at the ends of the chapters we've provided situational exercises and specific principles and tasks that you can do and discuss in your team right away.

Situational Exercise

Try this experiment with your leadership team: have a meeting about the material and content that is normal for that meeting—perhaps it is your weekly staff meeting—but end the content portion of the meeting fifteen minutes early. Now tell your team, "Okay, for five minutes write down as many gestures, tones of voice, or other subtle relational signals as you can remember seeing happen during the meeting."

After the writing time, let everyone talk about what they saw and heard.

You'll be amazed at how much more most of the women saw and sensed relationally—how many more facial and physical expressions of emotion, for instance.

First Principle and Task of Balanced Leadership

Principle 1: Gender intelligence and, therefore, gender-balanced leadership begin in the understanding that we are, in large part, hardwired to be who we are. This understanding begins a work/life process of nurturing our own nature and feeling personally responsible to help others nurture their own authentic gender qualities. When we open our thinking to science-based insight about gender, we take a first step in trusting both our own and the other gender's abilities, and we begin to expand into areas of gender intelligence that can lead to authentic and balanced leadership for both women and men.

Task/Actions 1: Begin the process of revisioning your leadership and management philosophy toward dealing with gender issues scientifically. Be open right now to wherever this revisioning takes *your* corporation. Also be open to where it takes you personally, and your leadership team as a group, including gaining an understanding of those individuals who are exceptions to gender "rules."

Summary

1. Gender and gender roles are not the same thing.
2. Gender is hard-wired, and can be understood scientifically.
3. Like any scientific principle, theory, or process, science-based gender study requires constant "lab" work, observation, dialogue, collaboration, adaptation—not stereotyping!
4. PET, MRI, and SPECT scans can reveal a great deal about differences between male and female brains.
5. Genetics research indicates chromosomal roots to our gender traits.
6. Actual and natural brain differences have positive implications for gender-intelligent leadership.
7. The terms *male brain* and *female brain* do not mean one brain for each gender; the gender/brain spectrum is quite diverse and includes bridge brains.
8. Balanced and gender-intelligent leadership is an achievable positive goal of science-based thinking regarding women and men.

2

Understanding How the Male and Female Brain Work Differently

I have found the brain science information truly fascinating, a real eye opener. I had always thought that, as professionals, men and women were more or less the same, except for a few personality differences. I woke up at 3 AM the morning after the workshop realizing all the differences I had either misunderstood or misinterpreted. I have to tell you, it really changed my view and my way of working.

—JOHN HUNKIN, FORMER CEO, CIBC WOOD GUNDY

IN A SEMINAR IN NEW YORK, TWO EXECUTIVES SHARED A STORY with our group. The woman was the CMO and the man the CFO of the same company. They had spent many years developing the trust they needed, all the while carrying on a recurring argument about male/female difference. This particular argument is what we call the "it's all about relationships" and "it's never about relationships" dichotomy.

The man's attitude was this: there's work to be done; relationships are a waste of time unless they directly serve the work; the more you get done in an hour the better; why waste so much time on relationships? It's unprofessional and even immoral, because it harms the workplace. Her attitude was this: there are always a few minutes available each hour for relationships; tone of voice matters (in other words, how you act with me and others indicates your character—and character isn't just about morality, it's also about subtle signs of caring and respect);

plus, relationships ultimately help the bottom line, so you're missing the truth about business if you think relationships don't matter.

His words to her often were essentially: "Facts matter, feelings are secondary."

Her words to him often were essentially: "Of course facts matter, but relationships matter just as much."

When we pressed this man to make sure not to exaggerate his position, he did admit that business requires forming and working through relationships—and, he insisted, "I'm not stupid, I know relationships matter, but most of the time, we just have to get things done!"

She responded: "Of course we have to get things done, but not from *outside* of relationships—we are *inside* relationships. They always matter, because they are the way we get things done."

These two executives were living out differences in the male and female brain that utterly impact leadership, all over the world. And these two executives were living out only the tip of the iceberg!

Three Primary Areas of Brain Difference

In Chapter One, we looked at how to use science to understand gender, especially how it hard-wired (on a broad spectrum). In this chapter, we'll look closely at the primary areas of brain difference themselves. We hope some of our scientific information and our anecdotal examples will make you smile. When we share this material with corporate leaders, we often hear, "Aha! I always knew that about men or women, but now I have the science to prove it!" Don't be surprised if you find yourself saying, "Wow, I didn't realize that. That can really affect our corporate team."

You may also find yourself at times saying, "Well, you know, some of what that piece of science proves does not apply to me—I'm exceptional in that way." How wonderful that will be!

There are three major categories of brain difference between male and female brains that ultimately impact every aspect of our workplaces:

- Differences in neural blood flow patterns
- Differences in particular structures in the brains
- Differences in brain chemistry

Brain research from all continents confirm these differences, which, as Columbia University professor of clinical medicine Marianne Legato recently put it, begin long before we're born. In her words: "Our sense of ourselves as either male or female is cemented into the brain after the first trimester of pregnancy." As we explore these differences with you, we will help you "get into each other's heads." You'll see how understanding the female brain better can help men do better at negotiation of contracts and making sales, and understanding the male brain better can help women rise in hierarchies. In both cases, the accommodations men and women make to brain differences improve their own and the company's bottom line.

Blood Flow Patterns in the Brain

Blood flow represents the neural activity in a brain at any given time. As our brains are living, working, leading others, loving a mate, being empathic, developing an idea, honing their innate skills, trying to relate to others, they generate different blood flow patterns. Sometimes this is called *neural activity* and sometimes *glucose metabolism in the brain*. What it means, simply put, is where the electricity is flowing among the cells of the brain.

SPATIAL-MECHANICAL AND VERBAL-EMOTIVE DIFFERENCES   One of the most confusing areas of blood flow difference is the greater reliance in the male brain on blood flow through spatial-mechanical centers in the right hemisphere, and the greater reliance in the female brain on blood flow through verbal-emotive centers in both sides of the brain. In the female brain, more neural activity occurs in the parts that think in and create words *and* in the parts that connect those words to memories, emotions, and sensory cues; in the male brain, more neural activity occurs in the parts that use physical and kinesthetic intelligence, as well as spatial mechanics and abstraction.

??? Did You Know ???

Gender Difference Can Be Misleading

Pointing out the possibility of brain differences in spatial processing got Larry Summers, the president of Harvard University, into hot water in 2005. He asked universities to include information on brain differences in their surveys and studies of why so many fewer women joined engineering faculty than men.

How things are said can be quite important, because if this brain difference is not dealt with accurately, it can keep women out of science professions. Our research in this area shows that boy's and men's greater neural reliance on spatial mechanics and abstraction does *not* mean women can't be engineers. Nor does it mean women are worse at math and science than men (another popular misconception).

Actually, in schools in the industrialized world today, girls are generally catching up to boys in their math/science scores, for a variety of reasons both on the boy-brain and girl-brain side of things, and also because of changes in the way kids are taught and tested. Further, the terms *math* and *science* are now too broad for what is really going on in male/female brain difference. For instance, in spatial manipulation, males test better than females, just as females test better than males in verbal-emotive functioning, but males and females test equally in numerical and quantitative reasoning, which is a primary key to math skills.

As more is learned about the spatial and verbal blood flow differences in the male and female brain, college engineering and science programs, as well as engineering and architectural firms, will find themselves more intrigued by women's brains, not less. For this to happen, however, a full understanding of spatial and verbal differences in assets will have to become honestly and fully discussed in our culture.

What's happening in the brain blood flow patterns that goes deeper than any stereotypes or simplifications? Recall that in Chapter One we introduced the way gender is imprinted onto the brain: first through genetics, then through hormonal surges in utero. That second step—the testosterone and other hormonal surges in the brain during gestation—directly results in different neural blood flow patterns later in a person's life. In her remark quoted earlier, Columbia Professor Marianne Legato is referring to this brain chemistry. Beginning in the early 1980s, neuroscientists began to prove that these testosterone surges compel the male neural system (body and brain) to *differentiate from* the female not only by making testicles and other characteristics of the male body but also by establishing a different formatting for the brain's future blood flow patterns.

One of the major areas of differentiation occurs in the right hemisphere. Testosterone surges in utero cause the normally female-developing verbal centers in that hemisphere to be supplanted by spatial-mechanical centers in the male. Quite interestingly, another similar surging of testosterone happens at puberty, which further develops the spatial-mechanical proclivity in the male brain. If you wonder why boys and men predominate in the playing of spatial, mechanical, aggressive video games, you're seeing the nature part of the nature/nurture answer—the result of these testosterone surges, first in utero, then in puberty.

Infant and toddler boys often tend to see physical objects (including dolls) as spatial and mechanical "toys," to be explored through spatial manipulation—if you give a couple of dolls to a toddler boy, he is more likely than a girl is to throw the dolls into the air or bang the two dolls together. This is spatial play—the result of more blood flow in his brain going into and out of spatial centers.

Infant and toddler girls, on the other hand, tend to see dolls as relational, emotional, verbal objects. Girls will tend to integrate these dolls into the hospital, house, or other relational game they are playing, talking to the dolls, generally *not* throwing them into the air or banging them together.

This spatial difference in male and female brain processes continues throughout life. When boys and girls grow up and become men and women who go to work, the difference can become achingly clear, as the women and men in a filmed experiment discovered.

??? **Did You Know** ???

Men Often Need to Relate, Learn, and Succeed Spatially

We were filming a typical day at an investment bank, and the men were tossing NERF balls back and forth. The women had to physically duck as the ball coursed by. The women wondered, "Are these guys intimidating me on purpose? Are they intentionally being jerks?" The men, oblivious to the issues caused by the flying balls, were in fact using the spatial object, the ball, to relate to each other—while tossing the balls comfortably, they solved problems, developed ideas, and even de-stressed.

You may have noticed in your own workplace that men often use a physical object, like a ball moving around in physical space, to focus their energy, bond with one another, succeed against challenge, create group cohesion, and work off stress. Men often want to do something physical and spatial in order to feel at home in the world. With more blood flow in their brains moving in and out of spatial centers in the right hemisphere, this is understandable.

Women often bond, build cohesion, succeed against challenge, and focus their energy by other means. To work off stress, a woman might say, "Let's talk—I just have to get this off my chest. . . ." After talking through something, she may notice that she feels much better. Women don't generally feel as compelled or drawn as men do to toss a physical object back and forth. It is understandable that women, with more blood flow moving through verbal centers and less through spatial centers, often prefer a verbal way of working things out.

If a female leader doesn't know about this, she might think—as did some of the women during our filming—that "the men are being rude to women." A man might think (upon hearing this reaction from a woman), "She's so sensitive—she'll never be a leader."

When we use this film in our workshop with the leaders, there are many "Aha!" moments—women realize their incorrect interpretation and feel better; they see that the men in the video had no ill intentions. At the same time, the men in the training become aware of the level of stress their neural way of being can cause their female colleagues. Once they understand, they and the women agree they do not need to eliminate the ball tossing from their workday, but they do need to be more sensitive and restrained in their behavior. It becomes common sense to respect each other both physically and neurally.

This might be a good moment to talk in your leadership team about the blood flow differences in spatial centers:

- Do you and your fellow leaders notice men throwing things at each other (pencils, paper airplanes), joking, or mocking each other, or hitting each other on the back, arm, or hand (to physically show appreciation)?
- Do you notice some men's eyes glazing when relationships are discussed, or a lot of words of appreciation or comfort are being expressed—do they perhaps reach for an object to squeeze, tap, or toss around?
- Do you notice men's arms, legs, bodies occupying more physical space around them than women's (using more of the desk, floor, or table than the woman next to them does) for their "things," their papers, their creativity and expression?

- Do you notice women relying more on trying to connect words to feelings and trying to show appreciation and bond with others by using words rather than quick physical or spatial gestures?
- Do you notice how much less women are apt to toss a ball or other physical tool between them in order to relate?
- Do you notice women trying to extend conversations rather than end them quickly, often using question endings like "Don't you think?"—questions that make relationships more verbal, less physical or confrontational?

We don't want to simplify everything to "words and feelings" and "physical objects and action," but store in your mind this blood flow difference in verbal-emotive and spatial-mechanical centers. We'll return to it all through the book as we continue applying brain difference to your workplace and keep moving toward the integration of gender intelligence and balanced gender leadership in your corporation. It's a big deal, because it is so misunderstood and so politicized that people can get fired for talking about it.

Yet as you read more, you'll see that talking about it from a real scientific perspective can lead to immense company growth.

GRAY AND WHITE PROCESSING DIFFERENCES Brain scans now show us that, in the same way that blood flows in the male and female brain to differently developed spatial-mechanical and verbal-emotive brain centers and pathways, blood flows differently in the white and gray matter of the brain.

Men have approximately six and a half times more gray matter related to cognition and intelligence than women have, and women have nearly ten times more white matter related to cognition and intelligence than men have. In all our brains, gray matter processes information locally in the brain, whereas white matter networks and connects information between different information processing centers in the brain.

Because of the gray/white matter difference, women tend to move more information among diverse brain centers. Men tend to localize information in one or two centers.

The gray/white difference is one reason men tend to excel in tasks requiring more local gray matter processing (they tend to like to focus on one task and one task only: "Just the facts, please" or "Don't bother me right now, I'm busy!"), whereas women tend to excel at integrating and assimilating information from distributed white matter regions in the brain, such as is required for greater language facility and greater multitasking.

The CMO and CFO at the beginning of this chapter illustrate this wonderfully. She is wired for the constant multiconnecting of fact-based and relationship-friendly work. She responds best to the talk *and* the emotions *and* the memories stimulated by both, *as well as* the accomplishment of the task at hand. He, on the other hand, is likely to find all that multiconnecting overstimulating. His brain is set up to stick with the thing he's doing and get it done, get it accomplished, not "waste time" with "needless" interconnections.

If you can, talk about this for a moment with your team:

- Do you see fewer men than women in your workplace thinking out problems in words attached to feelings?
- Do you see more men working without talk than women? People will often say, "Men are more direct and to the point," or they'll say, "Women are quite creative, but in their own way." These generalizations can be beginning points of good male/female conversation. Because they process white/gray matter information differently, men and women tend to gravitate toward different types of communication, concepts—even designs and ways of marketing or selling.
- Do you see women thinking about a number of design concepts at once, like jugglers, and seeking out a collaborative conversation (even via the Internet and texting) in which to integrate everyone's concepts together? You may see men frustrated and thinking they should figure something out independently, or thinking they've "got it" in one local area of the brain. They may find later that what the collaborative female brain has developed is equally successful and subtly different.

- As you look around the workplace, notice whether many of the women around you are asking open-ended questions, such as "What do you think about that?" Go farther by noticing that many times they are not asking these questions because they don't know the answer, but in an effort to build collaborative relationships on a team that will support multitasking and interconnection in the short and long term.

- Do you even see women losing executive power by asking "white matter" questions? For instance, do you notice a woman asking a "What do you all think?" question or something like "What about that issue could we benefit from discussing further?" that makes a man think, "Doesn't she know the answer? Doesn't she already know what to think about it?" Do you further observe the man actually restating her question as a direct statement, then presenting it moments later as if he himself thought of it? In this particular case, he may garner a group statement like, "That's a great idea!"

If you notice patterns like this in your team, talk about whether the woman has succeeded in encouraging verbal and group discussion at the cost of the recognition and reward she deserves—negatively affecting her own self-esteem and career advancement. Understanding a brain-based communication difference like this can lead to an executive team's greater gender intelligence and better management of assets, both through the woman's more careful choosing of when to be direct and when to focus on building consensus, and the man's working in greater partnership with her, such as asking, "Claire, what do *you* think?"

EXPERIENCE PROCESSING   In addition to the white and gray matter difference, there's a blood flow difference in the *cingulate gyrus*. This part of the brain, inside the limbic system in the midbrain, is the part that runs life experience around in our heads, as neuroscientists Ruben Gur and Daniel Amen have shown. Women have, in general, a more active cingulate gyrus than men. One result of this difference is that women's approach to life and to work is one of *constantly reassessing*. Far more than men, at any given moment women are running sentences, tones of voice, gestures, facial expressions, meetings, TV commercials, arguments with a colleague through this part of the brain. Men don't remember as much, process as much, run as much experience through the gyrus, so they spend less time internally processing, and thus can often be less contextual than women.

We observed a good illustration of this phenomenon when we facilitated a gender leadership program at a global professional services firm. We began by going over the data about retention of women and information from opinion surveys. The men in the room dug right into the statistical data, saying, "Look at this stat on the loss of women in the thirty-five-to-forty-five demographic. That's the key right there." Not surprisingly, many women in the room immediately said things like, "Yes, and the data is like that because our women feel constantly excluded from the informal network. Here are some examples. . . ." The women provided immense anecdotal detail, immediately, regarding each set of behaviors, including exact memories of time and place. The men were less able to remember and connect all of those contextual dots.

One reason for this tendency in women is the gyrus activity—women are more sensitive, in general, to the context surrounding information because they are processing it more constantly and completely than men, in general. Men are more likely to zoom in on what they think of as "the facts." Of course, there will be exceptions in these gender tendencies, but think about the full range of human assets you have right in your own boardroom: quite often, men are more adept at revealing the depth of your corporation's future through analysis of the facts and figures; many women can reveal the depth of your corporation's future through analysis of human context.

As boardrooms become more gender intelligent, it is powerful to watch individual leaders come together in working toward a balanced leadership model: in this model, a gender-intelligent male leader will not assume he has "gotten" everything that went on in the meeting—he'll ask his equal and trusted female partner what all the subtle signals were in that meeting. One reason is that he instinctively and somewhat humbly suspects that a trusted woman may be seeing more than he is about what makes people tick.

A male jury consultant told us, "I am good at reading faces and good at what I do, but I take this gender/brain stuff seriously. I try to work with women partners as much as possible—they see things I don't see." He understands the advantage of the greater cingulate gyrus activity in women.

There is also a disadvantage to the more active cingulate gyrus in women. Women and men need to be aware of it. Some women can get bogged down in relational matters—a possible outcome of the highly active cingulate gyrus (and other related brain activity). This can harm a career. Just as a gender-intelligent male leader might ask a trusted female colleague for help debriefing a meeting's contextual realities, a gender-intelligent female leader might ask a trusted male colleague to help her see what is and is not emotional or relational in nature—for example, she might need him to say, "That's not the issue—it's a side issue; here's what's really important."

As one female executive recently told us, "I hate to admit it, but I spend a lot of time thinking out problems that may not be problems. Sometimes these are 'problems' I have with other people, sometimes just issues I see in myself. I have a male assistant for a very good reason—to help me decide whether I'm overreacting or not to certain situations, especially among my relationships with men. I can't talk to most men about this—our corporation is cutthroat—but my male assistant is someone I trust with my life!"

As we spoke with this executive about her advancement in her company, we could see that she had a tendency to look too harshly on her own actions, not just the actions of others. As neuroscientists Daniel Amen and Ruben Gur have both concluded from PET and SPECT scan studies, this trait is common among individuals with a highly active cingulate gyrus. There are brain-related reasons why this executive, like many women who engage in multirater feedback studies, self-rates lower than men. It was liberating and career boosting for her to understand that men tend to rate themselves higher than their peers and even their bosses rate them, but female leaders tend to rate themselves lower, often beating themselves up for no reason.

Authentic leadership for this female leader joined with gender intelligence to make her less hard on herself and to help her understand her innate wisdom in relying on her male secretary for feedback. She gained a better sense of how to act, react, and even self-promote in her very competitive work environment—without becoming someone other than who she was.

REST STATES   Have you ever seen the humorous diagram of the male and female brain at rest? The male brain is nearly blank, the female brain immensely active. This bit of humor has a basis in reality! While doing brain scans at the University of Pennsylvania, neuroscientist Ruben Gur discovered that men's brains naturally go into a rest state more than women's brains do. Women's brains don't rest or deactivate the way men's brains do.

Overall, there is more neural activity in the female brain at any given time than in the male brain, as evidenced by 15 to 20 percent more blood flow, with more brain centers "lit up" in a scan of a female brain (see Figures 1.1 and 1.2). The male brain is more prone than the female to "zone out" or "blank out" during conversations or at times of exhaustion and stress. The male rest state can also manifest in "more activity" during an activity—but activity that is really about trying to keep the brain out of the rest state. For instance, you may have noticed men tapping pencils, tapping their feet, swiveling their chairs . . . they may well be trying to keep themselves from being bored or from zoning out; that is, they are stimulating their own brains in order to be fully present during a "boring" meeting. This is generally unconscious and not a slam at the meeting leader. It is brain wiring at work. The man is trying to keep his brain out of a rest state.

If women don't know about these neural tendencies, they may make a number of crucial misinterpretations. When men zone out, perhaps looking out the window while the women in the room are still maintaining eye contact and nodding, the female leader of the meeting may often presume the men are not taking her seriously. She will think,

"Men don't listen. Men don't care." But quite often what is going on is a simple result of the males' brain wiring—men not only listen differently (for example, holding less eye contact in general) but also sometimes need to just zone out for a moment, then bring their brains back to action.

An exciting way to get to know this brain difference in your own team is to observe men and women in meetings over a one-month period. See how many women in the meeting room are taking more notes, seeming more engaged, making more facial expressions—also tapping pencils less and seeming less "distracted." Take another look at the brain scans in Figures 1.1 and 1.2. You'll see how much less blood flow occurs in the male brain during the neural rest state. Your month of observations will probably reveal that men are going into rest states in these meetings more than women are.

When we do gender leadership programs in corporations, we show the PET and SPECT scans and analyze them with executives. Some executives say, "These scans have completely changed my understanding of meetings, negotiations, and work in general. Men and women are so amazingly different!" The neural rest state is one of the most amazing areas of difference. Both women and men leaders enjoy joking about "the rest state"; they also enjoy seeing a reduction in the level of misinterpreted behavior that follows a deepened knowledge of the brain pattern difference between women and men.

Structures in the Brain

Increasing gender intelligence and moving toward balanced leadership begins in understanding who each other really is. Using each other's strengths to help the whole team succeed requires using a strong lens to see into our own and our colleague's minds. The more we have the courage to do this, the more quickly misunderstandings move aside, and we learn the "gender skills" of the men and women we are working with.

We've looked at how blood flows differently in the male and female brain. Now let's look carefully at some of the structures of the brain and how they work differently in women and men. Some of the brain structure differences involve size and formation; others involve use.

THE HIPPOCAMPUS   Have you ever wondered why women generally can remember more physical and relational details than men, such as the color of a client's office, the kind of flowers they put out on display, as well as the emotional experiences each person seemed to be having on a given occasion?

The *hippocampus,* a significant memory center in the brain, plays a key role in women, as women constantly test out better than men (in general) at remembering the specific and minute details of interactive situations and events. Certain areas of this memory center are often larger in women than men, and there are often more neural pathways between the hippocampus to emotive and sensory brain centers in women than in men.

Gender-intelligent men will often trust what women "saw" during a contract negotiation. Studies completed all over the world, over the last twenty years, confirm that women in general read signals on faces better than men do; they are also better at reading gestures and other subtleties. Knowing this can lead your corporation to a balanced leadership gain: women often can remember later—during debriefing—more of what they saw during the negotiation, and thus interpret well the direction the negotiation may be going. You can use this advantage to help with next-day preparations in subtle and crucial ways.

An illustration of this occurred in a company responding to an RFP process. The company had a gender-balanced team in place when making the pitch to the potential client. Unfortunately, when they went into the presentation, they relied on two men, with similar gender styles, to complete the vast bulk of the presentation. As they were leaving the room, the two men high-fived each other, sure that they had won the deal. But the two women warned of what they had seen on the faces of the panel members: in fact, they hadn't convinced two crucial people. Their two male colleagues disagreed, saying, "What do you mean? We addressed every single point they asked for in the RFP."

The men were effectively and efficiently going through the agenda; the women were connecting to the faces, the moods, the metamessages.

When this team came together to decide whether there was a need for a second presentation, the men did not see one. They did not do a follow-up meeting, did not address concerns, and, to make a long story short, they lost the deal. In the postmortem, they found that the women had been right on the money: the two panel members identified by the two women had killed the deal. Not only had this company lost a $50 million deal, it was also out of pocket the $32,000 it cost to do all the research and prepare for the presentation.

THE AMYGDALA Have you ever wondered why men tend to get more "physically expressive" when they get angry? The *amygdala* is one possible reason. The male amygdala is larger than the female amygdala, and because this structure stimulates more activity downward in the male brain toward the brain stem (and thus more quickly into the physical body), and more often upward in the female brain toward talking centers, men and women tend to differ in their angry behavior. At the very moment men's bodies are feeling their anger and trying to expel it physically (and the male brain is specifically *not* producing words to deal with the anger), the female brain is becoming very verbally stimulated. The woman may be saying, "Tell me what you're feeling. What's this anger about?" Her cingulate gyrus and her hippocampus may be involved actively, tapping memories of errors she's made, running them through her brain instantaneously, internalizing and personalizing them; she may want to bring these to the male, but his amygdalic functioning should caution her. This is not the right moment. He can't "hear" her words the way she is saying them.

Workplace relationships involve conflict and anger (all relationships do), and knowing how different our brain structures are, and how interwoven the differences between structures are, we can better relate to one another. It is absolutely crucial to the contemporary workplace that men and women rethink their expectations of one another during conflict situations. A large part of gender intelligence and balanced leadership happens in this revisioning; GenderTool 4, in Part Two of this book, will focus on practical strategies regarding male-female conflict that you can put to use immediately.

Brain Chemistry: Our Neurochemicals and Hormones

Not only do male and female brains differ in structural components and blood flow, but they also secrete their chemicals differently. This chemistry difference profoundly affects leadership and, ultimately, everyday life. Differences in brain chemistry can initially be understood when we realize that males secrete more *testosterone* and *vasopressin* (aggression and territoriality chemicals) than women. For instance, a man will have between ten and twenty times more testosterone in his blood and brain at any given moment than a woman has. Females, on the other hand, secrete more of the brain chemicals estrogen, progesterone, serotonin, and oxytocin. Serotonin and oxytocin are less well known than estrogen and progesterone; serotonin, among other things, calms our impulses down, and oxytocin, among other things, is a bonding chemical.

At the beginning of this chapter, when you were reading about the blood flow differences in the brain, did you wonder why there are such differences in neural activity? Specifically, why do our genes include markers that set males up to toss objects like balls at or near each other in order to be relational, and females to try more often to talk to one another and make calmer eye contact to show their affection and authentic self? Indeed, in thinking about brain chemistry and gender, it's actually quite fascinating to ask, "Why has human history set males up with more aggression, spatial, and territoriality chemicals and females with more calmness and verbal bonding chemicals?"

The prevailing scientific theory looks back to hunting and gathering. This is what we did for a million years (agriculture started only about ten thousand years ago and industry about two hundred). Hunting is physically or psychologically aggressive (or both), it is spatial, it is not very verbal, and it includes long periods of neural rest states, while waiting for the hunted object to reappear, or at the end of the day, when the hunt is over.

Gathering (and child raising near home) includes the need to read more emotive needs and signals, less physical aggression, more eye contact, more verbal bonding, and more consensus among more networks of individuals.

Given this million-year genetic history, different hormonal baselines of males and females seem to have led to males in general tending to act more impulsively and less calmly than females; males tending to bond with fewer people, less verbally, in a given hour or day (or lifetime); males tending to fight over territory more than women; and males tending to act more aggressively and competitively in a given hour or day—as one executive put it, "over every little thing!" Of course there can be exceptions to this—women who are immensely competitive and men who are not—but in general you will find more "hunting" in the male leaders in your workplace than in the women. This mode feels more neurally and chemically authentic to men in general.

For fun, as well as to try to illustrate how a million years of history might still be present in our genetics and chemistry today, take a look at these scenarios with your team. For brevity, we have accelerated the conversation in each.

Scenario 1: Male Buyer, Male Seller

Seller: I see you're looking at the leather couch. Great choice!
Buyer: How much?
Seller: $4,500.
Buyer: Are you kidding me? I just need a couch, not a Picasso.
Seller: But look at the leather! It's from Italy.
Buyer: Yeah. Well, I'm busy—you gotta do better than $4,500.
Seller: Hey, I've got a wife and two kids; I can't cut my
    commission.
Buyer: So what? I'm divorced and I have three kids!

They'll banter back and forth; then if all goes well, they'll come to a deal. The men in this scenario are focusing on the final outcome of the transaction, with friendly competition over who is in the direst financial situation.

Scenario 2: Female Buyer, Female Seller

Now, if we play the same scene with a female buyer and female seller, the conversation might go like this:

Seller: How can I help you?

Buyer: I'm looking for a couch for my home office.

Seller: That will be wonderful. How big is the room?

Buyer: It's a small room, but I like the idea of a big couch across one wall.

Seller: Oh, that might work. What is your color scheme?

Buyer: Very simple; I think this light blue piece would work.

Seller: Will there be kids around? Because if there are you'll want something that is easy to clean.

Buyer: No kids, so the leather will be fine. How much is this one?

Seller: That's a beautiful choice. It's $4,500.

Buyer: I like it so much, but it's too much money!

Seller: Oh, I'm so sorry. Perhaps we can find something that suits you better?

Buyer: What about that one by the wall? It's a little smaller, but it would fit.

Seller: Great, let's look at that one. The price is going to be just right.

Women don't tend to go hunting right away for the goal. Their first step is often the building of rapport. In this case, the seller wants to know about the client and her needs. When it comes down to price, the seller does not try to convince the buyer; she apologizes as if the high price in some way puts their relationship at risk. The buyer looks at other options relatively quickly, without "holding on to" the bantering and competing that the men might tend to do more of.

Of course, these scenarios can go another way, with men being less competitive and women being less interested in rapport building. And certainly, when they do go the way we've described them, female and male approaches grow in part from how boys and girls are nurtured to act with one another. Yet, having said that, we add to our greater understanding of our colleagues by realizing the chemical origins of behavior in the genetic history stored in X and Y chromosomes.

For women, higher levels of the bonding chemical oxytocin can lead to a deeper interest in more complex bonding—it is natural. Similarly, although many boys are nurtured to become aggressive men, the original imprint of their negotiation and leadership style lies, to a great extent, in a chemical base for who they are. It can show up in something as daily as friendly competition during the buying and selling of a couch, and something as crucial to human survival as how males and females react to stress.

??? Did You Know ???

Men and Women React to Stress Differently

Neuroscientist Tracey Shors has recently shown, in her work at Rutgers School of Neuroscience, that the genders experience stress differently because men and women secrete different chemicals when stressed. Men will tend to use competitive and physical responses more than women, whereas women are more likely to try to talk through a situation. Oxytocin is one reason for this response. Here's how it works.

When humans feel very connected to someone or something, this feeling of bonding and connection comes—to a great extent—from oxytocin. Oxytocin is partly responsible for what biologists call the "tend and befriend" instinct, often contrasted with the "fight or flight" instinct. The higher the oxytocin level in a person's brain, the less physically aggressive the person is likely to be.

Because the female brain secretes more serotonin and oxytocin than the male brain does, women in your workplace tend to spend more time enjoying visual and sensory objects (such as flowers) on a desk or in a work space, and less time bantering with one another, or bumping the other person, or slapping hands in high fives. Women also tend to try to "talk out" their stress with more words, whereas men try to "compete it out" through ritualistic debating and competition with male peers and even with female peers.

We were doing some work with female leaders from Liberia and discussed the "tend and befriend" versus "fight or flight" instinct. One said, "That is so true. When the war was on, the men rushed out to fight. The women gathered in smaller groups closer to home." Civil war is a far more extreme experience than life in the boardroom, but because the underlying brain functioning is the same, you can see equivalent behavior in a corporate setting. During a stressful conflict in the boardroom, some men will withdraw, but others will turn the meeting into a turf war. This is generally not because they are jerks; they are responding naturally to threat and stress.

A similar illustration of this biochemistry appeared when we did work with the Los Angeles Police Department around preventing harassment and discrimination. When we presented biochemical and scientific information about males, females, and stress, the head of a region, a man, had an "Aha!" moment, which he shared with the group: "Is this a reason why women officers are often so good when we send them into conflict situations? I can think of five recent situations where women were able to calm down a situation involving firearms rather than getting into a shooting."

This officer may well have been seeing biochemistry at work and gaining information on how to value differences and deploy those differences to achieve objectives. As the whole team discussed these differences, its members decided to look at how they use personnel and when—who would lead and who would follow in a specific high-stress situation. They gained, in short, gender intelligence.

Misinterpretation of intentions between women and men, especially when both genders experience stress, can get in the way of leaders and corporations. In your own leadership team, do you notice a man who, when stressed, tries to compete not only with men but also with women? What are the consequences of this natural, chemical response to stress in your leadership team? A particular man you know may need immediate coaching—if the man overdoes the stress-responsive competition, especially with a higher-oxytocin female leader, she may feel offended, and he, in turn, may feel she's unable to relate to him. Lacking gender intelligence, he may not understand how to alter his behavior to accommodate her, and she may not understand how to interpret his signals.

A female executive told us a story about her feelings of ambiguity and confusion regarding male competitiveness in her workplace. She recalls beginning her career saying things like, "I don't want to do the corporate softball game. It's just a bunch of guys posturing and hitting each other." Even before she understood brain chemistry differences, she knew the value of gaining access to the power particular men had, but she didn't realize the mistake in downgrading the softball game as a part of male relational importance. She didn't see that this safe, testosterone-based male battleground of relationship was a way into power.

Once she learned about chemical differences, she realized that, sure, she didn't need to become a man, but she had to find a way not to reject how males worked off stress and related to others. This female executive very smartly learned to play golf (a game that, as it turned out, she enjoyed greatly). Now much of her relating to male leaders took place during golf games. She knew that a lot of women just wouldn't want to play golf or softball, but for her it was a good match. When we asked if she felt more or less authentic by learning golf and relating to men during a competitive game, she reported that in the first few months she had felt less authentic to herself, but as she came to enjoy the game and the new way of de-stressing and gaining camaraderie in her executive team, she felt more authentic.

Women like her, who seek balanced leadership, can find the brain chemistry differences daunting at first, as if "crossing over" to the male way of being is a way of losing themselves; if, however, they become skilled at working within male chemistry, and if they find points of connection and enjoyment with game-playing, competitive, aggressive men, they often feel, in the long term, that they have not lost themselves—their femaleness—but instead gained access to, as this executive put it, "a secret kingdom of male power."

Male Banter Is a Secret of Male Power

A male executive told us this story:

> I went one night to play poker with the guys—we get together a few times a year, eight of us—and I had just been having heart trouble, a small heart attack, difficulty breathing, rapid heart rate. I had been in the emergency room two days before, and now I was on a Holter monitor.
>
> When I told the guys about my situation, they could see I was frightened and stressed, but you know what they did? After being sympathetic for about a minute, they spent the rest of the night saying things like, "Don't beat Joe, he'll have a heart attack," and "Are you okay, Joe, with my aces? I don't want you dying right here."

Joe and the guys laughed through this banter. He concluded, "I was stressed about the whole heart thing going into the poker game, but these jokes were just what the doctor ordered!"

Joe's story is iconic of the power that male bantering and one-upping brings to male life and leadership. It is a constant testing of strength and weakness, a constant pushing of limits so that males remain always at the top of their game. This kind of male bantering feels comfortable to competitive men, but can confuse less competition-oriented women (and men). Although some women get very good at the give-and-take of it, many women see it as unnecessary or at least immature.

Gender-intelligent men learn not to use aggressive banter when it would hurt feelings, but the fundamental truth remains: male-to-male relationship building is, in general, different from female-to-female relationship building. The constant honing of competitive verbal skills in men is actually a secret of male success that gender-intelligent women should look at more closely. The woman who learned golf not only learned a game, but came to learn the kind of male bantering skill that she might have learned in childhood only if she were brought up with four or five brothers. She learned new gender skills, which helped her advance her career.

Is it only men who try to toughen each other up? Of course not! Often in our seminars, women will look back at their own childhood moments of verbal meanness, rumor sharing, and even personal battles they had with girlfriends. They will notice that they were competitive with other girls. After learning about biochemistry, they will wonder, quite rightly, "Was our method of competing a more oxytocin-based way that girls try to gain a competitive edge?" Indeed, they'll realize that both girls and boys were trying to make each other tougher, though in different ways (and certainly they'll realize that both males and females can take things too far).

Just as gender-intelligent men will partner with female leaders in negotiations, gender-intelligent men will watch how women compete with each other—especially the verbal methods women use for one-upping, criticizing, "putting the knife in," as one woman executive called it—and gain new insight. Brain chemistry and hormone-based studies do not show women to be noncompetitive. They show, instead, different ways of competing, with men spending more time focusing their energy on hierarchical competition—in part because their bloodstream is more constantly flooded with aggression, competition, and territoriality chemicals—and women spending more of their time competing through verbal interactions in smaller groups.

In this book, we'll constantly alternate between teaching secrets of male power and secrets of female power. Respecting how female leaders often read social situations and negotiation signals better than men is a way of learning secrets to female power, and using them. So too is taking the time to understand not only male ways of competing, but also the ways females compete. Especially for men working with female leaders, it is crucial to listen carefully to and become as facile as possible with women's verbal styles. Simultaneously, if you are on a team of mainly men, you will need to look carefully at whether your team's interactions are so heavily "testosterone-laden" that they force the few women on your team out of the team—or force them to form their own small group, competing against one another and against the men. Situations like this end up damaging leadership teams. In the short term, men feel comfortable with other men, but in the long term the men lose the assets of the women, who leave the team for a place that better understands the way women think and relate.

??? Did You Know ???

Men Have a Biochemical Cycle Too!

Do men have testosterone cycles? It's generally known (even if often misunderstood) that women have a hormonal and biochemical cycle, but did you know that men have a hormonal and biochemical cycle too? It is not a monthly one, but a daily one. Most important to work life, men's moods are affected by it!

Male testosterone surges when a man wakes up in the morning. Then, in the hours from around 9:00 AM to around 11:00 AM, there are further surges of testosterone through the male bloodstream. Gabrielle Lichterman, CEO of My Hormonology, a corporation that studies both male and female cycles, has observed that during this period males are especially apt to be aggressive negotiators, to be ambitious and determined, to feel a competitive edge and confidence. Males also test out better at spatial reasoning during these testosterone surges than they do later in the day, when testosterone drops.

Does every man feel this every morning? No. Many other factors can operate in a daily life. But all over the world, male testosterone cycles are similar, so it is worth observing the extent to which the male cycle is operative in your leadership team.

Similarly, it is worth observing how men act in the midafternoon (between 3:00 PM and 5:00 PM). Male testosterone now tends to be quite a bit lower. Men are likely to be somewhat more "pliable"—more agreeable to suggestion, less aggressive and defensive. These late afternoon hours are post-lunch, siesta hours, so all of us—male and female—may well become a bit sleepy during this time, but in men, specifically, low testosterone contributes to lowered competitiveness and aggression. If you are working late, it is also worth remembering that male testosterone rises in the evening but then diminishes again around 8:00 PM. At this time, oxytocin rises in men, replacing some of the diminished testosterone. Men tend to be more likely to talk about feelings and resolve conflicts if the conflicts are not large, and do not entail a major outlay of energy. This time period is one in which male brains are trying to go to rest states, given the tiredness from the day, so large conflicts generally don't get resolved now, but lower testosterone and raised oxytocin mean another window of pliability.

Burning Question: Do Women Have to Become Men to Get Ahead?

Very often in trainings and coaching, both women and men will follow their understanding of biochemical and other brain differences with a burning question: "Because corporations are inherently such competitive environments, don't women have to become men to get ahead?" One female leader in an executive team workshop put it this way: "It seems like guys are set up from genetics and from boyhood to do impulsive things, maybe fail in the short term, but in the long term to climb to the top of aggressive corporations, while we women are still in the position of deferring too much to others, taking too few risks, and getting left behind in the long term—unless we become men!

"I know that's not the takeaway you are going for," she concluded, "but some folks, learning these differences, could think it is. What do you say?"

This executive said what everyone was thinking, and she said it in a wonderfully challenging way. There is indeed a possible, inherent disadvantage to women's relational activity in the highly competitive corporate world. Women are often less hierarchically aggressive, lower risk, less confrontational, less competitive. That lack of aggressiveness may not serve the typical female as well as the typical male's "do anything to get to the top" way of doing things. His higher self-ratings (even if undeserved), his ability to banter, even about death, his constantly recharging testosterone cycle—all can lead to the supposition that his authentic leadership style is inherently better for corporations than hers. Certainly, thirty, forty, or fifty years ago that was almost always the case; and in many parts of the world it still is. Women, wanting to succeed, either had to hope that corporations would suddenly change—becoming less competitive, lower-risk places (something few corporations did or can do)—or women had to become female men—more brash, more impulsive, more . . . each of us can fill in what we want to here, depending on what we feel "men" or "male executives" are like. Women had to become, in other words, "more like men."

In the early 1990s, Barbara coined the term *third sex phenomenon*. She used this phrase to help facilitate dialogue about why women were training themselves to act like men and, in the process, becoming neither man nor woman, but a "third sex." This approach was working for some women, she knew, but at the same time, many women felt a deep dissatisfaction—the third sex phenomenon tacitly reinforced the idea that the "male way" was the "right way" for corporations, and the female way of leadership was defective.

Now, as we move farther along in the new millennium, brain sciences and the new gender intelligence are affecting corporations in another way, one that directly follows from knowledge gained about the kinds of things you've learned thus far in this book. Corporations can not only deepen their understanding of how men and women lead differently but also act immediately to promote female leaders in ways that maximize women's strengths and increase the company's bottom line.

In Part Three of this book, we will focus completely on retention and advancement of women and men in areas in which they are under-represented. After deepening your understanding of brain differences, and then helping you integrate that understanding into your executive team through ready-to-use tools, we will provide a number of ways you can attack issues you might face in your corporation regarding gender promotion, discrimination, or loss of talent. By the time you finish this book, your answer to the burning question regarding women's advancement will be, we hope, the deepest and most practical answer the new millennium has to offer.

Moving Forward

As your team looks more deeply at "Where do we go with brain differences in our corporation?" you'll be unconsciously and consciously looking at how to balance testosterone and oxytocin, gray matter and white matter, process and product, inclusion and exclusion. Indeed, you'll be looking at the most important issues human beings face in any sector of life. Work life is human life.

Balanced leadership for women and men begins to clarify itself through this focus. As you leave this chapter, it is important, if you are a man, that you develop a greater sense of care for women's difference in hierarchy development—look more carefully at the exact capabilities a woman brings, without telling her she can't be respected until she becomes like you. For balanced leadership to work, men don't need to let women off the hook in competition (a woman still must prove herself), but the gender-intelligent man needs to look more carefully at the myriad ways in which a woman is already proving herself, and gain respect for those. And gender-intelligent women need to make sure the corporate hierarchy sees what they are accomplishing, especially via their own relational and functional style of leadership.

At the same time, if you are a woman, you need to consider whether you are misinterpreting male behavior. Men do listen, but differently. Men are trying to build relationships, but in a way that you may not recognize. Female leaders can learn to give men the benefit of the doubt, for their intentions normally are good, even if their behavior seems odd from a female brain perspective.

In Chapter One, the task for the executive team was to take in the scientific approach—to add it to the dialogue in the corporation and, if possible, make it a foundation of the gender dialogue. As you end this chapter, your task now is to practice specific honesty about specific people (this includes self-awareness). Where do you and the people around you fit on the gender/brain spectrum? Who are you? Who are they? What are your gender assets, and theirs?

Altering workplaces and workplace expectations toward balanced leadership depends on creating a foundation for this asking and answering. We hope this chapter and the previous one have helped you create that foundation. As you move forward now, we hope you'll get involved in regular discussions in your executive team. The next chapter will give you even more grist for the mill. Commit, as this chapter ends, to a brave honesty of awareness between genders—gender intelligence.

Situational Exercise

In your next executive team meeting, think through experiences you have had in which a female tendency is a strength; then think of a parallel situation in which a male tendency is a strength. Talk about these. Perhaps you've noticed that a man tends to be task oriented whereas a woman might spend more time on context— how might that play out in a specific challenge you confronted recently in your team?

Here are two examples—cases we have seen that you can use to begin dialogue.

A male project leader was warning the team that with a deadline looming, they had to focus to hit the month-end target. A woman spoke up saying she was worried finance wasn't on their side (which had happened on another project), and that they should schedule another meeting with them. One team member said, "What has that got to do with anything? We can just tell them what to do." But the team leader was savvy enough to recognize that the woman might be picking up on something he was missing. He chose to squeeze in another meeting, and this paid off. The project indeed began to reach the goal more quickly and smoothly.

A female consultant was very worried about a banking client. She had seen the treasurer whispering something to a colleague and was concerned something negative was going on. Her male colleague talked her through it, saying, "We really don't know what was said, and if there is an issue it will come up in our next meeting anyway." In the end, she realized that she was reading too much into the situation, and his calm focus on the facts helped her get back on track.

Second Principle and Task of Balanced Leadership

Principle 2: Deeper understanding of male/female differences leads to a deeper individual and team awareness, with each gender learning from and relying on the other's gifts for corporate success.

Task/Actions 2: Work together as an executive team to list and get to know each other's personality and gender assets. Use gender coaches and trainers as advisors as much as needed, especially if clear gender issues show up—you are not involved in an easy task here, and there are pitfalls.

Summary

1. Three areas of brain difference particularly affect every moment of work and life.

2. Our female and male brains are equally smart, but can be smart in different ways.

3. Men tend to be more spatial-physical in their relating and leadership styles than women.

4. The male brain periodically goes into a rest state, whereas the female brain tends to be more constantly active. Awareness of this can help men and women navigate many aspects of the workplace, especially meetings.

5. Men tend to compartmentalize more brain activity and focus on one task, whereas women are more natural multitaskers, especially in relationships.

6. Male aggression is helpful in many ways in leadership, but female capabilities, such as rapport building, are equally important. The balance can be very powerful.

7. Female leadership assets can specifically improve the productivity, morale, and bottom line of a corporation.

Understanding How Men and Women Lead Differently

> For much of the twentieth century, most scientists assumed that women were essentially small men, neurologically and in every other sense except for their reproductive functions. That assumption has been at the heart of enduring misunderstandings. . . . When you look a little deeper into the brain differences, they reveal what makes women women and men men.
>
> —LOUANN BRIZENDINE, M.D., AUTHOR OF *THE FEMALE BRAIN*

WHEN DID YOU REALIZE THAT YOU NOT ONLY FELT DIFFERENT from the other gender, but that you might actually *lead* people differently?

Was it while you were growing up and experiencing differences between boys and girls? Was it while living in your family home and observing your parents' differences?

Was it in your own adult life as a parent, perhaps? Whether you were realizing "I'm a mother" or "I'm a father," you may have intuitively felt the particular qualities of your gender in that role.

Or was it in your community, on a soccer field, at a philanthropic program, or at an event of some kind where you had to adapt to a male or female leader there in order for the event to go well? Wow, you might have thought, "he/she is in some other place than I am, but we have to get along."

Or was it in the emotion-charged environment of your love relationship or marriage? When did you intuit that your mind worked in many ways differently from your spouse's?

Each of us probably has many moments when we sense how differently women and men feel, think, and lead.

For Jennifer Allyn, a managing director at PricewaterhouseCoopers, a moment of realization came with an insight regarding the female tendency to "apologize" (and male tendency to not apologize) in her leadership team. She told us: "I noticed differences in how women relate to hierarchy. Women tend to apologize as a way to diminish hierarchy, not because they are really sorry. For example, they may say, 'I'm sorry, I don't have that document, can you get it?' Well, that's just being polite, it's not meant to be some sort of admission of fault. Men are less likely to apologize, and women may interpret this as being rude. They may think 'Surely, he could have said he was sorry.' It's not that women are right and men are wrong, but men and women lead differently."

Manifestations of Brain Differences in Leadership

Over the last two decades, we have gathered on-site evidence of how brain differences can affect behavior among leaders in the workplace on an everyday basis. Let's explore this material together now. As this chapter helps you explore how differently men and women behave specifically in their leadership roles, please always remember the bridge brains. The gender/brain spectrum is vast, and there are exceptions to every construct. Remember, too, the third sex phenomenon and the role of culture. While exploring this chapter, you may gain additional insights on parts of the brain you learned about in Chapter One or Two. The information and boxes in the next few pages are set up specifically so that you can easily discuss the bullet points with your colleagues, executive team, and managers. The material leads to a final section on core leadership differences. As you complete this chapter, you will have gained even greater practical insight into specific principles and tasks necessary for the development of gender intelligence and gender-balanced leadership.

Interpersonal Relationships and Relational Styles in Leadership

The brain differences we have described—in white/gray matter, the cingulate gyrus, the amygdala, the hippocampus, the verbal-emotive brain centers, and blood flow in male/female brain activity during specific tasks—also lead to specific *leadership style* differences. Authentic leadership for women is somewhat different, in many cases, from authentic leadership for men.

Female leaders tend to be more *interactive,* wanting to keep interactions extended and vital until the interaction has worked through its emotional content. So much more sensory and emotive information is processed through female brain blood flow that female leaders tend, more than men do, to seek more interactions in a day.

Men leaders tend to be more *transactional in their interactions*; that is, they are unconsciously thinking "I am in this relationship to give something in order to get something." Once the transaction of the interaction is complete, they tend to move away from the interaction and back to their more solitary task.

Female leaders tend more toward *participative* teams—they tend to try to find ways in which colleagues are complementary. It is probable that higher oxytocin levels affect this leadership quality—the more support women build around them, the lower their stress level, and the more effective they may be as leaders.

Male leaders tend toward a strong/weak *hierarchy*: they tend to see colleagues as potential competition, and they focus on who is in charge—and even who can be weeded out. It is probable that higher testosterone levels affect this leadership quality—the more competition certain men experience, the more comfortable they are.

Of course, in both the participative and the hierarchical leadership styles, the higher the hormone level in the individual, the more extreme he or she might be. And in all this, culture matters greatly as well. *And* there are always exceptions to these gender styles, and exceptional moments in which each of us acts differently from what people might expect.

Both women and men *collaborate*, but often in different ways. Men tend to include more testing of each other's ideas against worst-case scenarios (male leaders tend to lace competitiveness into more steps of the process than do female leaders).

With greater processing in the brain between more brain centers, female leaders tend to see *possible connections* between each person's different ideas—and try to find developmental elements in the connectivity. Each piece, they suspect, may be a part of a relational whole. Often, it must be proven to them that a piece is flotsam and can't be connected together with another piece. Men, on the other hand, tend to want to move more quickly to the ultimate goal and to spend less time on each piece or potential issue.

Female leaders enjoy independent work and even solitude, but in general, male leaders will tend to spend more time in a day working *alone*, without friendly words to others. It is often a personal challenge for a man to see if he can "solve the problem himself" or prove himself by doing the job well *himself.* Women are more likely to enjoy solving problems *with others,* for many of the brain-related reasons we just described.

Female leaders tend to be more *inductive* in leadership problem solving than men. This is about listening, hearing viewpoints, building a sense of what to do in a woman's mind from hearing all voices around her. When she knows what to do, she's not as worried as a man might be about proving it with data: she can already see that it works. One reason for this intuitiveness may be that she has a larger *corpus callosum* connecting both hemispheres of the brain; she is not guessing as much as a man might be regarding a relationship, once she has collected all the information she needs.

Men leaders tend more toward the *deductive* style in their problem solving. This involves more risk-taking guesses, but it also relies on more linear data and proof. Men will often see a solution and act on it, but expect to be challenged constantly on the data, the proof. Men will tend to take these challenges less seriously than women, and as par for the course. Men often take a more "guess, then prove" approach, and can be quite intuitive, but at first they may not feel as confident in their intuitions (if they are being honest with themselves!) as women tend to be, especially regarding relationships.

In the long term, male leaders tend to define themselves more than women do by their *accomplishment and performance* (sometimes men can feel that their career accomplishments are all they really have) than by their success at *keeping personal or workplace relationships intact* (women are proud of their hierarchical or product/design accomplishments, but also define themselves by being relationally literate).

Female leaders are also, in general, more reluctant to toot their own horns than male leaders. As Jennifer Allyn of PricewaterhouseCoopers told us, "A brain-based leadership difference I see constantly in the workplace is that women are reluctant to brag about their accomplishments. They feel the work should speak for itself and want to be recognized for the work without having to draw attention to it. They feel blowing their own horn somehow diminishes the meaning of the recognition they get."

Management Styles

Many of the brain differences between male and female contribute to specific *management style* differences.

- Male leaders tend to be more *prescriptive* in their management—they will prescribe, direct, tell people what to do more aggressively, in general, than women do (obviously, some women are exceptions to this rule!).
- Female leaders tend to be more *descriptive* in their management—they tend to describe what they are looking for, and spend more time detailing to employees—and hearing from employees—how to accomplish the goal. It is probable that they spend this greater time in relationship management because they have up to double the verbal capacities of men in their brains (particularly the

greater connectivity between the verbal capacities in the frontal and temporal lobes and the emotive experiences they are having in the limbic system).

- In conflict management, men tend to seek out more *direct conflict* than women (of course, individual personality, as well as upbringing, can factor into conflict seeking or avoidance). Because of their aggression hormone reliance, from early in life males seek out and experience contest, conflict, and disruption and try to shape their own personal power assets through confronting the power of other males in hierarchies. Most males get a lot of practice with this!

- Although certainly many men are conflict-avoidant with other men, males who usually show no aversion to conflict can become conflict-avoidant, or even relatively ineffective in conflict, when facing workplace conflicts with women. Because avoidance of conflict between women and men can actually be counterproductive to executive team success, this is an area of gender intelligence we spend crucial time on in our programs. A conflict resolution tool for women and men is included in Part Two of this book. Female leaders tend to feel their work life disrupted by direct conflict, so they tend to accomplish more in behind-the-scenes conflicts. With higher oxytocin levels and lower testosterone levels (such as greater internal push toward continuity of relationship and less push toward disruption of relationship), and even though women will indeed say nasty things about each other, they will generally try to hide them so that at least a semblance of relationship still exists.

- Because women remember interactions, including conflicts, longer than men, men may perceive that women are holding on to a grudge, and thus distrust female managers.

- When judging employees, women tend to be more forgiving than men are of others, especially men who fail.

A partner at an accounting firm summed up some of the most clear management style differences she sees everyday. Gender intelligence, she noted, requires her partners and employees to go beyond recognizing differences to "really appreciating men and women for who they are. I see women looking for more input than men. Sure men do collaborate, but I see women doing it more. I also see women being less apt to defend their positions in public. Another difference I see is that female leaders sometimes take on too many responsibilities. They find it harder to set boundaries like, 'No, that's too much, I won't do it.'"

As you'll see more fully explored in Chapter Eight, companies have significantly increased bottom lines by gaining gender intelligence in these management and leadership areas and by creating balanced leadership benchmarks for both genders on their leadership teams.

??? Did You Know ???

Men And Women Lead Meetings Differently

When management turns its attention to meetings, you'll often find the following to be true:

- Meetings tend to be run differently by men and women—men use fewer words to describe things, in general, although they tend to take more airtime in a business situation (compared with at home) and spend less time getting everyone else's verbal opinions!
- Female leaders tend to look around the room for more verbal opinions than men do. They also tend more than men to want data fleshed out with "the human factor."
- Female leaders tend to let people speak longer to make their point than male leaders do.
- Men tend to interrupt more. Not only is interrupting a competition and dominance behavior, but many men, especially those who tend to be more right-brained—more

spatial and less verbal—find it neurally frustrating to hear a lot of words. They often interrupt and need help managing conversations better.

- Men tend to be more directive and more direct in their input and requests. Women often tend to ask others what direction they want to go in, and they accept more oblique references to how a process might be furthered. This can be seen as a lack of confidence instead of simply a gender difference.

- Male leaders tend to have shorter memories for conflicts, emotional battles, and emotional stresses from the last meeting than women do. With a less active cingulate gyrus, and less time spent in the limbic system in the processing of emotions, men are less likely than women to remember specific situations and the relational details about looks or tones of voice.

A Core Leadership Difference: Approaches to Being in Charge

In looking at how differently males and females lead based on the biology of their brains, we have built toward understanding how differently male and female leaders lead their corporations, teams, and colleagues. These leaders can appear at any level of a company. Let's take a moment now to look at the highest executives. Both men and women can be top dogs and, not surprisingly, our research shows that (with exceptions noted, of course) they lead at the top differently.

As we summarize the basic differences in leaders—some of which we have discussed in previous sections—remember that at the most senior levels, all of what we have said in the previous two chapters may well be amplified by the personality of the leader—to get to the top, you have to be very good at putting yourself confidently into the daily stress of leadership, whether you are male or female. But our research shows that women often embody senior leadership status differently than many men do. This difference is hard-wired, and it's part of gender intelligence, balanced leadership, and gender evolution as a whole.

Because senior leadership used to be defined only as male, let's start with basic characteristics we've found in male leaders. *Male leaders* tend to

- Bond with coworkers in *short bursts* of connection, both physical (a pat on the back) and emotional (a word of praise), or through goal achievement that is less tied to words and emotions and more to action and competition than that of female leaders (men's lower verbal-emotive abilities and higher testosterone may well be the biological reasons for this).
- Focus on leading workplaces and hierarchies through *order assessment, pattern thinking,* and *ritualized action.* Male leaders will tend to care less about minutiae of workplace needs, but care more about larger structures and tools the corporation might need for future survival.
- *Downplay emotion,* even at the risk of hurt feelings, in order to *play up performance.* Males are chemically and neurally directed toward immediate rewards from performance, and they often prod—and sometimes even humiliate or shame—coworkers in this direction.
- Promote *risk taking* and *independence* of the employee. Many female leaders also are very independent thinkers, of course, but in general, just as male biology compels many fathers to push children toward separation from caregivers and urge them to "grow up!" faster than moms do, male leaders tend to assume independence in others, and consider it weakness on a coworker's part if he or she needs "to have me hold her hand."
- Expect and enforce discipline and *provide contests and tests of skill.* Male leaders at the top tend to be more competitive than nearly anyone around them, especially in their assertion to others that being able to compete in tests of skill against others is the key to future success.

- Teach coworkers to *fight against personal and group vulnerability*. With less of the male brain's blood flow devoted to emotional processing than the female's, males in general, and male leaders in particular, tend to either deny emotional vulnerability or problem-solve it quickly. Emotional vulnerability stimulates high cortisol in the male—his stress hormone—and he uses his most efficient tack against that high-stress hormone: he shuts down his emotions.

- Guide the coworker to sacrifice his or her own *thinking and feeling* in deference to *authority thinking* until the coworker has *proven* him- or herself to be strong enough to become authoritative. Male biochemistry sets up male leaders to want others to prove they should be respected. There is also some sexism involved here: the male leader will monitor a recently hired female leader for many months and even test her until she proves herself strong and worthy. He may not do this for as long a period of time with another man.

- Direct a coworker's search for self-worth in the larger corporation through specific tasks and actions—that is, encouraging less feeling introspection and more *immediate action*. Males tend to try to help the coworker *feel stronger* even if the person does not feel better in the moment. Male leaders tend to care less about whether a person feels good. Male biochemistry sets males up to tend to want obvious shows of strength, above all, from others (though not shows of strength that threaten his dominance!).

Female leaders can be like males, and some female leaders can be "even more male than a man": the third sex. Anything is possible, and we probably all know women who have even modeled their own behavior on a particular male leadership style in order to survive. At the same time, our research shows that female leaders tend to

- *Bond with coworkers by extending conversations in exploratory ways*. Women tend to interconnect data and share common experiences. If one woman mentions her experiences working with IT, another woman might immediately jump in to share an experience having similar patterns. Men do this as well but not to the same degree.

- Provide as much *hands-on connection* to the coworker as possible. Given their higher oxytocin levels and greater verbal-emotive ability, women are more likely than men to try to ascertain the exact needs of a person, sensing how morale needs impact productivity on a daily basis.

- Emphasize *complex and multitasking* activities, actions, team development—expanding leadership into various tasks and away from dominance by one task. They discover a panoply of possibilities for a product, as well as within a worker's untapped capabilities. With a brain that cross talks between hemispheres constantly, women tend to value multiple connections.

- Work constantly toward helping others (especially men) express emotions in *words* rather than just in actions. Greater verbal-emotive brain activity stimulates this (as well as the following attribute of female leaders).

- Search for a method of *direct empathy* when someone's feelings are hurt ("How are you feeling? Tell me about it. What happened?"), even at the expense of other current goals.

- *Relinquish personal, daily independence* in order to be cognizant of other's needs. Female leaders are more likely than male leaders to adapt their schedule toward concentration on a person's immediate needs; their higher oxytocin and more active cingulate gyrus help them to be more attuned to the specific needs of many individuals at a time.

- Promote the development of skills and talents in coworkers through an emphasis on *verbal encouragement* and praise. Females' higher oxytocin and reliance on verbal encouragement often lead them to issue lots of praise, not realizing that many men are suspicious of too much praise.

- Try to help the coworker resolve emotional conflicts and stresses so that the whole bonding system can *feel better.* An individual's immediate sense of distress or anxiety triggers oxytocin in a woman, which can direct her to try to quickly defuse obvious conflicts, more so than her male counterpart.

??? Did You Know ???

Gender-Intelligent Leadership Throws Out Old Stereotypes

In a financial firm we worked with, there were two executives in the bond trading division—one a man, one a woman, both highly successful. Their strategies for success were quite different—the man honing straight in on the biggest investors and going for the big deal, the woman talking to many, many investors in a day, winning many small deals. In terms of numbers, their overall results were the same—they were equally successful.

When they lost a deal, however, their expressions of frustration were very different. The male leader was famous for smashing phones. His staff would count how many of these very expensive phones he destroyed in a year and joke as to whether he had a good or bad year based on the number of ruined phones. For many people in the firm, this trait was a plus; it showed how passionate he was.

One day the woman lost a big deal and broke down in tears. This is something you will now recognize as a typical example of a gender-based difference in behavior that might well be based in prolactin differences. No big deal, right? Unfortunately, the people at the firm didn't know about the science—and they badly misinterpreted the behavior. They were worried that she was beginning to break down under the pressure. They thought she had reached her limit. The backroom chatter started saying she was falling apart, and she quickly picked up on this misinterpretation. She began thinking about leaving this firm—her loss would have been a real blow, as she brought in a lot of money.

Fortunately, the leadership team on the trading floor went to work on becoming gender intelligent, providing support to both her and the very angry male leader, and generally clearing up misinterpretations of what is "weak" and what is "strong." This work as a team saved them a lot of money—they retained this very talented woman by supporting her in dealing with stress in her own way.

Balanced Leadership

The end result of learning about hard-wired gender differences in leadership patterns is not just understanding, but also practical action. As you read the characteristics of male and female leaders, did you feel an instinct toward action rising in you? Did you hear a voice saying, "One set of gifts just might be incomplete without the other. How can my company maximize both sets of leadership gifts?"

Imagine a workplace with only males leading it. Maybe you've been in one. When we ask executives and managers to tell us about such environments, we hear things like, "It can become like a jungle," "Winner take all," "Too much testosterone!" One executive told us about an engineering company, his previous employer, in which all but two executives were male. "The place had extreme communication problems, a total lack of mentoring, and severe retention issues—not just the women, but talented men were leaving."

Imagine, also, a workplace with only females leading it. You may well have experienced a workplace in either category. (Businesses that typically include more women leaders are publishing, the cosmetics industry, and social services.) The most common words we hear from men who work there: "I'm the only male executive on this team and I experience frustration with the way things get done; I prefer to use a different, more direct approach."

Leading Differently: The Success Story of Pam Gomez Gil

Pam Gomez Gil, a senior manager and executive with a number of technological companies over a span of thirty-five years, has been asking questions about male and female leadership for over thirty years, and living out answers. What she accomplished to support her corporation's bottom line while practicing gender-based authentic leadership shows a gender-balanced reframing in leadership—one that values both the male and female leadership style. Her corporation understood the inherent advantages of the female style of leadership.

Pam told us about a specific assignment at Digital Equipment Corporation in which she achieved significant success while exercising her female leadership qualities:

> With no intention to compare my style to the two previous male leaders of this product line, I simply did what I knew best, not even considering to emulate or "turn myself into" a male leader just because I had been promoted into a "classically male" leadership position.
>
> I was promoted to business manager for a product line in the Digital manufacturing site, taking on a business that had low performance and was considered a failure in the plant. The product had been in production for fourteen months; the new design had been received well in the marketplace. It was an innovation at the time: a controller system which connected the mainframe computer system to the storage devices, playing "traffic cop" by routing data automatically to available space on tape or disks and making it instantly available for recall.
>
> But the product had struggled in manufacturing: quality performance was extremely low, production output wasn't meeting requirements by more than 50 percent. There were angry internal customers who were constantly waiting for product to show up so that external customer orders could be merged and tested, only to finally receive units and have some fallout for quality issues, putting them further behind.
>
> My solution to the problem was to take the focus off the output and any other numbers. Instead, I worked with my team (all men) to focus on *documenting* the production process in more detail, and then getting full compliance to the *process* on the production floor.
>
> In three months the quality of the machines started to improve. In six months we had improved product output so that 75 percent of orders were delivered on time and quality improved from 60 percent good the first time out to 75 percent. By the end

of the year, quality was at 95 percent, we were meeting all order rates required, and our long-term reliability had doubled! All the other metrics in the business came up accordingly: production cost dropped, fewer worker's comp issues reported, absenteeism improved, etc. It became a satisfying place to work.

At the end of the first year during my performance review, my boss (male) confessed to me that he had been told to hire me by his boss, partly because his boss felt my track record in the plant was good in other areas, and partly because he was forcing my boss to gender-integrate his otherwise all male staff. My boss indicated that some of the senior engineering managers had warned him that hiring me would be a disaster: "You can't put a woman in charge of an important production line."

During this confession, my boss said that based on the outstanding performance improvement and the positive feedback he was getting on "his" department, he complimented me significantly in my review, gave me a hefty raise, and verbally told me he would hire me for any job, anywhere!

My success story came from some good luck (right place at the right time) and perseverance in *my* personal and female assets. The men who had taken the position before me approached things in what I see as being a very "male" way of doing things. I approached things in a more female way, a way more focused on maximizing relationships and the "process."

As a woman leader and mentor to younger women now, I see balanced leadership as working best when we are aware of gender differences, and maximize them. I believe that I as Pam Gomez Gil—both as a person *and as a certain kind of woman*—was the right person for this particular job.

Sure I faced the usual gender obstacles, and the male staff was initially concerned that I wasn't going to focus on the output numbers themselves. As they got to know me and realized that I wasn't patronizing them nor asking them to work so differently that they couldn't use their assets, *they got with the program.* Each staff member was responsible for an area of the process to focus on, ensuring that the documentation was right and that the employees were trained and could execute correctly. I got the product-oriented men to focus on process, and the nonverbal men to work with me on documentation. Simultaneously, I let each of them decide their own methods of getting it done, by teaming with their employees, working the detailed documentation, etc.—optimizing their individual work style and assets. By asserting my own style according to my instincts, I was able to show that the end result was achievable in more than one way, while making the area a much better place to work. My staff and I worked together according to our assets and succeeded.

Also, I want to say I worked hard not to "become a man in order to lead men." My strength area is in managing the process that gets everyone to the end product. This is my nature, I guess. In thirty-five years in the technology sector, staying with my nature was my best asset.

Pam's story speaks for itself, doesn't it? She and her company put gender-balanced leadership to work. She and the executives who hired and helped her followed the science-based approach to gender and used that approach to look carefully at and be aware of the "nature" of her gifts. This approach is not flawless, and it involves some generalizing, but it sure can work! Had her corporation not valued her way of doing things, it would not have reaped the benefits of increased profits.

Transforming Your Team

To help you nurture and challenge all possible talents and assets available to your leadership team, we will now move more deeply into the realm of practical solutions, helping you bring together female-brain assets and male-brain assets. The tools and applications you'll encounter in Part Two can help your corporation in two key ways:

- By training men and women in the diverse assets of the other gender group so that they are more sensitive to and more able to relate to that group.
- By creating a "balanced gender team" approach to leadership itself. With the new tools, you as managers and executives come together to use, in a balanced way, each person's natural assets.

This requires a "meeting in the middle" between how male leaders and female leaders tend to operate.

To make these things happen, successfully, your corporation may need to transform its team to meet the needs and use the assets of both women and men. Let's start the transformation process right now.

A Pause for Breath

Like the brain differences discussed in Chapter Two, for the material in this chapter to be useful in the development of balanced leadership in your corporation, your people need to discuss each section! Before you move on to the tools in Part Two, take a moment to pause, breathe, and spend time looking specifically at the leadership differences around you—enjoy them, see the exceptions, and let your own intuitions and talents come to bear on each one. Tell your own stories with your team.

We like to start discussions about gender in leadership with basic questions that take things head on. Through these, a team will often slide right into some of the others we've noted. Here are some discussion starter questions:

"So . . . what do you think? Do female leaders tend to multitask, with more attention to the details of each of the many separate tasks? And do men tend to focus on the details in a single task? How have we seen this in our workplace?"

An answer given us by Dave Roth, VP of engineering at Vivato Systems, was both incendiary and entertaining. He said, "Let's face it, if we want someone to make sure every 'i' is dotted and every 't' is crossed, we look to a female engineer/VP. Men are just sloppy." You can imagine, that really started a discussion!

Sometimes discussion starts out with joking and stereotyping and with feelings of discomfort, but it generally moves on to the deeper elements of difference. If you have any fear that your own team discussions need coaching or help, seek that help! Gender discussions *can* go badly—they need both tough and tender nurturing and facilitation.

Another discussion starter: "So, have you noticed male leaders tend to get more irritable more quickly than women when their concentrated task is interrupted? Like, for instance, Jim gets totally frustrated if I come up to him while he's buried in his computer. . . ." Now a name is being mentioned. Here again, it is crucial to work together as a team and get help and mentoring as needed. It's sometimes tough for men and women to keep a sense of humor and get along in their marriages and their families, much less the workplace! Leadership teams can be as close as marriage and family, and both a gender-intelligent sense of humor and a gender-friendly sense of respect are crucial.

As you try "discussion starter questions," move through the lists of differences we noted earlier in the chapter. Cover the relational differences, the management differences, and the communication differences. You may well find yourself saying something like, "I'll bet that's a result of the cingulate gyrus." Let the brain facts be part of the fun, even though you aren't trained in the neurology. Let them help you without limiting you. Take notes, even keep a journal of your thinking and experiences.

Try This
Use the Words of Leaders Like Yourself

Here are statements by leaders like yourself who are involved in transforming teams by deepening their understanding and use of gender intelligence and balanced leadership. These statements are composites from media reports and our training work with corporations. As you read these, you may find it interesting to discuss how the statements can help illuminate, in your own corporation and team, how females and males tend to lead. You can use some of these words to explain what you are thinking. These leaders have articulated key issues powerfully.

A female leader (from a media report):

> Is my leadership style different from a man's? That's a tough question for me to answer—so I asked my management team for their thoughts. That simple act, they told me, pretty much answered the question. They agree that my emphasis on group communication, on soliciting their ideas and opinions, is a major characteristic of my management style. They also say it's why they think I'm a good leader.
>
> Is this a distinctly "female" trait? The members of my team—all of them male—seem to think so. Does it work? I suppose it does. Indeed, I will be brash enough to suggest that the culture of my sports company has changed under my leadership—and changed for the better. Now the emphasis is on sharing ideas, communicating them throughout the company, and reaching common goals.

A male leader (from a media report):

> The chairman of the consumer goods company I know often talks about a major product line he introduced that flopped. It's not that he likes to brag about his failures, but that he wants to encourage risk taking. And he goes a step further. He knows which people in the company are taking the big risks, and he sits at their right hand and helps them along. I have even seen him be the last supporter of people who tried to make major changes when those changes didn't go well.
>
> Everyone else was against them, but he stood beside them.

A female leader (from a confidential journal entry):

> My observation is that men tend to make the changes easier and somewhat more "final" when they switch leadership teams. Their conditional view of love allows them to change

teams and very quickly invest their loyalty in the new team. Women can have a harder time of making this change. Women need to work on this if we are going to succeed at the top levels.

My personal experience with this phenomenon is an incident where a product line (a "business") was going to be transferred to a plant on the East Coast. The West Coast team was initially disappointed and even angry because the performance of the business was outstanding within the plant, and the team felt like they were being punished for "doing it right." When the team was broken up and dispersed to other businesses in the plant, the women established a lunch-hour or after-work meeting place to keep the relationship going. The men were sporadic in attendance and eventually disappeared from the effort.

The women had a hard time understanding why they were forgotten by the men, when it had been such a good team—wouldn't they just want to find a way to keep it going? Although some of the men remained friends with me, I found over time that if I didn't make the effort to call them or arrange a lunch, our relationship died. When we would run into each other in another setting, the men would be very cordial and want to talk old times—until they had to get back to work. Stepping too far outside the boundary of the new team seemed to imply to them that they would be deemed disloyal to the new team.

This difference between men and women can impact networking styles and expectations and the ability to work well together quickly on newly formed teams (which is the trend in modern corporations). While women can form new teams very quickly, they will sometimes do this only on the surface. They feel a sense of loss of the old team for too long, and it can bog them down in making the new leadership team successful.

Moving to Part Two

The first three chapters of this book have focused on understanding, from a scientific perspective, the brain and biological differences between women and men. We've focused first on the science, then on the differences themselves, then on how they manifest in the workplace, especially in leadership. We've worked hard to always acknowledge exceptions to rules and to retain a diverse vision.

We are on a journey toward a full vision of how to develop balanced leadership for the twenty-first century between men and women at work. We hope that, as you move out of Part One into Part Two, you have been able to shake off past stereotypes and hindrances to understanding the people around you. We hope you have deeper insight into the women and men you work with. We hope, too, you leave Part One with specific principles, tasks, and actions in mind.

Situational Exercise

For one week observe the gender dynamics in your meetings and then talk with two people—one man and one woman—about what you have observed. Come back to your next executive team meeting ready to share experiences, thoughts, and feelings about these differences. If needed, set aside time for professional development and training in gender intelligence for your team.

Third Principle and Task of Balanced Leadership

Principle 3: If we are committed to principles of authentic leadership, our corporations need both male and female assets in frontline, middle, and upper management, and at the highest CEO levels. As we look together and specifically at hard-wired differences in the area of gender leadership, we can achieve a level of mutual respect that makes possible greater innovation and advancement of talent.

Task/Actions 3: Notice the specific leadership style of each person around you, and notice how well you fit (or do not fit) with the gender style of each leader. Discuss each issue that arises; in doing so, get help as needed. Start your assessment by spending most of your time on strengths and much less on weaknesses in the other gender's leadership style.

Summary

1. Both women and men lead, supervise, and manage others effectively, but in different ways (ways that can easily be misunderstood).
2. Males and females are hard-wired, not just acculturated, to lead one another differently.
3. Men tend to be more transactional in their management style than women.
4. Meetings are an obvious area of male/female difference—men and women tend to experience and lead meetings differently.
5. Men and women often lead from the top differently.
6. Male and female leaders are already effecting change in corporations all around us, including perhaps in our own.
7. Frank and honest discussions of gender styles are key in executive teams, just as they are key to making marriages work.

PART

The Tools

Putting Gender Intelligence to Work Immediately

While it's true men can sometimes be more comfortable working with men and women with women, just like Japanese can feel more comfortable working with Japanese, for instance, or French people with others like them, it is actually by working with people who are different from you that you gain new value—men with women, Japanese with French. We're different. In learning to work together in the difference we can create the best future for our corporations.

—CARLOS GHOSN, CEO, NISSAN

GenderTool 1

*Improving Your Negotiation Skills
with Both Genders*

I can tell you, if I want the best deal for my client, I have to pay
attention to what works best with each gender, and there are definitely differences.

—CANDICE FUHRMAN, CEO, CANDICE FUHRMAN AGENCY

MUCH OF YOUR CORPORATE SUCCESS DEPENDS ON HOW WELL you or other
leaders do in negotiating deals. Little negotiations happen on a daily
basis; big negotiations make or break businesses. You have probably
learned from other resources some of the subtleties and good habits of general negotiation. This first GenderTool will add a gender
perspective—and increase your negotiation skills with women and men.

About Our Gender Tools

This chapter is the first of four GenderTool chapters, set up so that
you can immediately put four practical tools to work in your everyday
work life. These tools have been developed over the last two decades
and taught widely in corporations around the globe. They are based
on an understanding of the science of gender difference and its

application in workplaces like yours. These GenderTools can be used in a variety of ways: as exercises, scenarios, awareness tips, and to-do checklists.

The four GenderTools in Chapters Four through Seven work best for executives and managers if the whole leadership team discusses them (as you've done the previous chapters), but we've set these tools up in this book so that you can put them into effect as an individual, too, even if your colleagues aren't on board yet with the gender-intelligence transformation you are seeking.

The Science of Gender and Negotiation

As with every aspect of leadership we've looked at in this book, the human brain is the seat of negotiation, and men and women bring many similar and many different brain assets to the negotiating table. One primary area of assets (and differences) is in reading faces and other behavioral signals during the negotiation.

??? Did You Know ???

The Mind of the Negotiator Can Be Mapped

Whether you are male or female, your brain does the work of negotiation in this way:

- The visual and aural centers (seeing and hearing) pick up cues from the folks sitting around the table with you.
- These centers perceive the signals, creating a perceptual representation in the temporal lobe.
- Those perceptions are fed to other parts of the brain—the amygdala is a primary receiver of these signals, in part because negotiations are stressful, and the amygdala handles some of your stress emotions.

- The amygdala associates the perception with an emotion you feel, stimulating an emotional and verbal response in your body and in other parts of the brain.
- Your skin conductance, your autonomic sweating response, your smiles, your frowns, and many other physical manifestations occur as neurophysiological responses to the signals.
- There are feedback loops everywhere in this process, with neurons flooding your verbal centers and everything else!

This is a short list of what happens; you can probably see immediately how all this can happen differently in men and women who lead and negotiate:

- Women pick up more sensory cues than men do, so their brains tend to create more emotional perceptions. Thus women need to process more internal signals—one reason why negotiations with female leaders can take longer.
- A man's amygdala sends fewer signals to a less complex verbal center and more to spatial or calculative centers—one reason why men are often data driven and not complexly emotive in negotiations.
- The facial recognition activity in women's temporal lobes, amygdala, and elsewhere in the brain are more revved up than in men; thus women will pick up more facial cues to what others are feeling and thinking.
- Men tend to carry more territoriality and aggression responses in their amygdalic functioning than women; they can thus go for the jugular more quickly than women and push more aggressively for shoot-the-moon outcomes.
- For women, negotiations are more often about relationship than men realize. There is so much emotive and relational content moving through the female brain that men risk losing a woman's respect if they don't understand how she is operating during a negotiation. If a woman is having a negative experience with the other negotiator, she can be

very decisive; it could be the deal is dead, even if she politely sits and listens for a while. Once male negotiators understand this, they usually don't have a problem adapting.

- Simultaneously, female negotiators risk losing men's respect if they don't look into men's eyes and realize, "I'm becoming so relational in this negotiation that his eyes are glazing over and he's detaching. I'd better get back to the facts."

What Executives Have Said About Gender and Negotiation

What male/female differences have you noticed during negotiations? Here are some significant things that other leaders have observed. You'll notice they fit well with the brain differences. They also provide tools that you can take advantage of.

Only in the last 10 years has the male-dominated world of venture capital opened its doors to women—and only because it's had to. Highly competitive markets can't afford the luxury of discrimination. That said, whenever you mix women and men—and then add money—interesting things are bound to happen.

When a man is sitting across the table from a woman who is sitting on a pile of money, the situation can get uncomfortable—especially since it's every venture capitalist's job to say "no" a hundred times more often than she says "yes." That's why I'm always careful to put people at ease, to connect with whoever is on the other side of the table. Any venture capitalist needs to know what it's like to wear an entrepreneur's shoes. But that's especially important for women.

Early in my career, I had a meeting with an entrepreneur whom I tried to help—with my opinions, not my money. Later I discovered that he had called me a "bitch" who liked to tell people what was wrong with their ideas. My first reaction was to think that he wouldn't have said that if I were a man—and I got mad. My second reaction was to say, "How stupid of me!" I was giving him feedback that he had no interest in. I've learned that you should wait for people to signal that they want honest feedback before you offer it.

—DARLENE MANN, ONSET VENTURES

Darlene's insight into men (and her very smart lack of overreaction to this man's aggression) improved her negotiation talents. She didn't hold a grudge, she "got" what this man was doing, and she engaged in the chess game of negotiation without letting too much feeling invade; at the same time, she was altogether herself, negotiating in the way *she* was born to negotiate.

I believe that "gathering" is at the crux of how women view and use power differently from men. I've had lots of experience with business negotiations—an activity not unlike hunting, since it's fraught with conflict and casualties. Men have tended to demonstrate a "go for the kill" mentality. They try to get as much as possible through pressure, intimidation, and the sheer desire to defeat at any cost whoever is sitting across the table from them. Women have tended to prefer searching for common interests, solving problems, and collaborating to find win-win outcomes.

It's not easy to find the freedom to operate with a "gathering" style—even though there is plenty of research documenting that collaborative approaches offer the best chance of producing high-quality results. But in the real (read: male) world, collaboration is often viewed as a sign of weakness. So unless you're the boss, collaboration is risky. That's why, over the last few years, I've focused on helping to build entrepreneurial businesses in which I can be a leading participant. I want the freedom to work in ways that work.

—SHARON PATRICK, MARTHA STEWART LIVING OMNIMEDIA

Sharon's approach—to form her own businesses in order to circumvent male-dominant approaches—is useful for many women. She noted also how tough it is to negotiate with males who simply do not respect the female negotiating style. These males may succeed, in the short term, in pushing women away, but in the long term—certainly in the next decade—it will not serve them well; as they ill-adapt to women's approaches and to the female brain, they will lose out in crucial ways reflected in the bottom line.

> Differences in negotiating styles can linger in the background. If I don't think about it, I am prone to think, "There's no difference between women and men." But then when I just take a few negotiations to observe things, things lingering in my mind appear very clearly.
>
> For instance, I've noticed over and over again that female agents and publishers use more guilt and emotion, whereas men tend to just go for the data. Men present the numbers more, and make a case for why a certain dollar amount is appropriate. Women will tend to talk longer about how much a publisher is doing for my client and how little the client is doing . . . and therefore how much less money they should pay.
>
> I also notice that women are constantly reading my face. Until I learned about the brain research on male/female difference, I didn't put my finger on this, but now I see it. Women are searching my face, reading signals. Men seem to be getting their signals from me in other ways, maybe in nonverbal stuff I'm doing. They aren't as occupied by eye contact and facial signals.
>
> I wouldn't say women or men are better at negotiating, but they are different, and each has his or her own way to the outcome.
>
> —CANDICE FUHRMAN, LITERARY AND FILM AGENT

Although it's true that every leader is an individual, and not all gender typing fits everyone, our focus groups have corroborated what these negotiators are saying. In our focus groups, both male and female leaders said for men it seemed like *everything* was a negotiation, from where to each lunch to what to order on the menu! At the same time, the groups revealed that men were rating women's negotiation skills lower than their own (and women were also underrating themselves) because, mainly, it was the male negotiating style—data driven, highly aggressive, filled with banter, even abrupt—that was unconsciously being used as the highest standard of negotiation.

Something important gets missed when women and men both undervalue the women's negotiation-through-rapport and overvalue men's negotiation-through-data-and-banter. What mainly gets missed is the effectiveness of both, *in the right circumstances*. The future of corporate success (especially with women occupying 50 percent of the workplace) lies in women and men both becoming gender intelligent in negotiations.

Applying Balanced Leadership to Negotiations

Gender intelligence, like emotional or intellectual intelligence, is important to every negotiation. You will have to decide how important it is in a given situation. As you incorporate the gender intelligence in this book, consider adding these balanced leadership tools to your toolbox:

- Put together a team of negotiators that includes both women and men.
- Pick the right person to lead the negotiations. Do the strongest gender assessments you can on the people you are negotiating with, and plan strategically which women and men to have involved in negotiations—and which parts of the negotiations they should handle.
- Read gender signals clearly during any negotiation you observe or participate in. Check both perspectives, intuitive and factual. By reading male and female signals more clearly, you'll know where you stand, how successful you're being, and what other tools you need to bring to bear—including other gender assets—to develop appropriate rapport, data, and outcome.

As you work in your team on this gender negotiation tool, talk about the following five specific areas of focus in any negotiation (essential details about each of them follows). Then talk about the different gender intelligences, behaviors, and follow-through of women and men in each area.

- Preparation
- Personality

- Use of data
- Rapport building
- Intended outcome

Preparation. It can be useful to have both women and men creating the preparation materials. They will each see and feel different needs in the material. Can your team see an immediate need for this? Or maybe you can think of a past need that didn't get filled—perhaps a negotiation that might have gone better if this piece of gender intelligence had been fulfilled.

Personality. It can be useful to decide—based on who you are negotiating with—whether you need more than one gender in the negotiating room. If your own personality, for instance, is somewhat set and rigid, especially in its gender, a negotiating colleague of the other gender might be in order. Carefully ask, "What are the gender assets of each of our team members in negotiations?"

Use of data. If you are a female leader who is great at a lot of things but not as good with the data as a man on your team (or vice versa), you might want that "data geek" to take point on laying out data during the meetings and negotiations. Can you see a way to do this division of labor in your next negotiation?

Rapport building. Are you spending enough time during negotiations in building rapport with the other company and team members? If, for instance, you are a data-driven man who is bad at building rapport, can you rely on a coleader woman (and, of course, genders can be reversed here) to help you build rapport?

Intended outcome. Quite often, the intended outcome for men focuses on task completion "even if we need to step on a few toes." Female leaders can use the singular task focus of their male team members to help drive past barriers and not let an emotional response derail the negotiations. Female leaders' intended outcomes generally include maintaining good relationships. The attention women pay to relationships can help men avoid unnecessarily creating opponents who obstruct the current or future negotiations. Have you factored these relevant gender differences into your next negotiation?

To-Do Checklist—For Your Team Right Now

❏ Don't leave this chapter without making a decision about someone or some company you are presently in negotiation with. What one step toward balanced leadership in negotiation should you institute *right now* that will positively affect your present negotiation?

❏ Does the group you are negotiating with include males and females? Should this inspire you to include more males or females in yours?

❏ Does the group you are negotiating with include no females? Would you gain advantage by bringing a woman leader to the table with you—an advantage the other team will not have?

To-Do Checklist—For Men

❏ Include more women than before in negotiations, as providers of insight, interpretation, relational energy, visioning, and negotiating power.

❏ For a month, watch how female leaders work. Watch how they negotiate. Pick out five strengths you hadn't seen before. Focus on them. Try to emulate them, to some extent, where useful.

❏ Respect women's negotiating styles for what they are, even if they irritate you or put you off. There's something going on that you may need a few months to appreciate.

❏ When possible, mentor women around you in how to best negotiate with men. If you are really good at what you do, ask one or more women if they want your help. You understand that male world you live in better than they do (at times). Help them. They will help you.

To-Do Checklist—For Women

❏ Mentor other women in your negotiation strengths (and mentor young men, too).

❑ Take very little personally; remember, you are negotiating in a world of aggression and territory. To prove yourself, you may need to keep coming back to the table until you are respected.

❑ Look for corporations and systems that will support your style of negotiation, and when you leave an unsupportive system, make it clear why you did so.

Should women become more like men to become good negotiators? Should men become more like women? These questions will be asked for decades to come.

Ultimate success in all spheres comes when we remain ourselves but learn from others. Both women and men should learn from each other, and both women and men should be valued in a room. You saw this need to learn from each other played out in the "$50 million lost deal" story in Chapter Two. Men and women can "become like the other" in the small ways that matter, but we are more likely to succeed when we remain, at our core, naturally and authentically who we are, adaptable but not lost to ourselves. Gender intelligence is and always will be about tapping into the skills inherent in each gender until we feel comfortable in the room with those skills—and able to gain allies in those skills when we don't feel comfortable.

GenderTool 2

Running a Gender-Balanced Meeting

Meetings are one of the most important activities a company engages in during a workday. They are also a crucible for male/ female relationships. We've discussed this many times in our company, how meetings hold up a kind of telephoto lens to all the "stuff" that's going on between women and men.

—ROBERT COLE, CPA, CORPORATE CONTROLLER, KXLY BROADCAST GROUP

BALANCED LEADERSHIP BECOMES ALL THE MORE POSSIBLE when you build your gender intelligence up to the point where you can fluidly run a gender-balanced meeting. One interesting and amazing brain fact to take into your meetings involves the hormones testosterone and oxytocin. Males, as we know, are driven by testosterone, having up to twenty times more of this aggression chemical in their bloodstreams and brains than women have. Women are more actively driven by oxytocin. These brain chemicals are directly affected by meetings. It happens in this way:

Meetings raise our levels of cortisol—the stress hormone. When women's cortisol levels rise, they tend to secrete more oxytocin. Their brain system says, "You need to decrease your stress level now by 'tending and befriending'—protecting relational cohesion, keeping tension levels down, making sure social connections are secure."

When men's cortisol levels rise, they tend to secrete more testosterone. Their brain system says, "Assert yourself independently, interrupt, make sure you are aggressively known, mark your territory, take risks, challenge social cohesion if that will further the ultimate goals of the system or your own place in the system."

We bring very different sets of chemistry and brain functioning to meetings! No wonder meetings can be so complex.

Yet they also can be focal points in our corporate transformation and gender evolution—places where balanced leadership is very possible, and very needed.

For Women—Understanding Men's Behavior in Meetings

- Because a man's brain frequently goes into rest mode, men may keep themselves awake by what might appear to be fidgeting—clicking a pen, tapping, looking away, and the like.
- Because men's brains are not wired as well as women's to constantly multitask, men may become more frustrated when others have multiple conversations that don't seem focused.
- Because men's brains often process fewer words than women's brains process, men are more likely to zone out if discussions become lengthy or wordy. The appearance of this "zoning out" can make it seem like the man is not interested or doesn't care.
- Because men's brains are wired to be more aggressive, men will sometimes dominate a meeting. The meeting leader often forgets this and does not involve all participants so all opinions are heard.
- When meetings become stressful, male testosterone levels rise, creating increased competitiveness and aggression—a deeper fight-or-flight mentality. It's impossible to overemphasize

how our brain chemistry affects us. Socialization as children matters, yes, but some of what you see in meetings is biologically wired (and very unconscious).

For Men—Understanding Women's Behavior in Meetings

- Because a woman's brain is wired to cross-connect information from both hemispheres, women are more likely to move from what appears to be one topic to another that seems unrelated, though they may actually be "connecting dots" that very much need connection during a project.
- Because women's brains are wired to be less competitively aggressive and more fostering of interdependence in a group setting, a number of women in a meeting may feel unvalued if their opinions and views are not specifically sought out.
- When a meeting becomes stressful, women's oxytocin rises, stimulating them away from competition and toward a tend-and-befriend mentality, which seeks social cohesion. This can "shut down" their assertiveness or put it into a kind of rest state. If leaders don't realize this, they will not help women voice their ideas during stressful meetings (and the company will lose their brilliant ideas).
- Because women are generally wired to be more attentive to process, the gender-intelligent leader is challenged (and often forgets the challenge) to set a pace and establish tacit and overt rules that both allow adequate discussion time *and* keep the meeting focused and moving forward.

For Women—Challenges and Checklist of Solutions

We hope you are inspired by all you have read to alter the way you do meetings to accommodate both the brains of women and the brains of men. Here is a short list of what you may need to do.

To be heard and taken seriously

To-Do Checklist:

❑ Use concrete words targeted to specific outcomes.

❑ End fewer sentences with an upward (questioning) inflection.

❑ Ask what he thinks, rather than what he feels.

❑ Compliment specific achievement outcomes.

❑ Make sure to use the art of repetitive approach: keep coming back to a suggestion you have, even hours or a day or two later—don't give up if you believe in it!

❑ Use positive reinforcement more than negative criticism.

If you are seen as out of control and unfocused

To-Do Checklist:

❑ Connect as much of your conversation as possible to the company's strategic priorities.

❑ Use fewer—and well-targeted—words; try to provide essential information only.

❑ When tangential conversations take place during a meeting, return to the purpose of the meeting.

❑ Publish an agenda for the meeting. Decide beforehand what outcomes are desired.

❑ Monitor overreaction; get help if needed.

For Men—Challenges and Checklist of Solutions

If you are seen as aggressive and dictatorial

To-Do Checklist:

❑ Listen more carefully; stand in the other's shoes.

❑ Repeat back key elements of what's been said to you.

❑ Use appropriate speech; control anger.

❏ Don't discount anyone's opinion—listening doesn't mean agreeing.

❏ Compliment participants for contributions, when you can sincerely do so.

Note: In this part of this GenderTool, as in all of these tools and exercises, it is crucial at times to substitute individuals for groups. For example, we've put dictatorial leadership under "For Men," but if you are a woman who leans toward being dictatorial, the same to-do checklist may work very well for you.

If you are seen as exclusive, not inclusive

To-Do Checklist:

❏ Seek opinions from both male and female participants.

❏ Have an intracompany female mentor assist you.

❏ Facilitate consensus by asking questions like "What does everyone think of that?"

❏ Monitor your own overreaction; get help if needed.

❏ Apologize, when warranted, more frequently than you now do.

Improving Your Meetings: Using Ten Essential Gender-Balanced Management Skills

When our team has studied meetings from the point of view of gender balance, we have found that focusing on these ten skills helps meet the needs of both genders.

Skill 1: Be a Complete Meeting Leader

A complete meeting leader is one who plans, facilitates, and follows up. As a leader you need to take seriously your role as planner *and* facilitator of an interactive process that sets the goals needed for the company's competitive edge. This combined emphasis on both process and goals helps satisfy both male and female brains in the meeting.

If you lean too much toward preplanning agendas but lack facilitation skills, you'll tend to lose women; if you don't preplan, but just shoot from the hip in a meeting, you'll tend to lose men. Generally, your own personal meeting-leadership skills are enough right now to have gotten your company or team to its present point—but to go farther, you may need to get help from mentors or coaches to improve your abilities in meeting planning, meeting facilitation, or post-meeting follow-through.

Skill 2: Set a Gender-Balanced Frame

The most efficient meetings tend to begin with a statement of purpose, review of the agenda, and alignment on intended outcomes. All collaboration and competition concerning ideas follows within the framework set by this beginning, so that both males and females are on the same playing field. If purpose, agenda, and outcome are not established, you are more likely to lose the ideas and talents of shy men, one or more women, and either women or men who just feel left out.

Skill 3: Make Meetings Adult Places

Meetings need not be a completely sedentary or boring experience—they aren't a negative stereotype of a schoolroom or a lecture from Mom or Dad. Use of empowering humor is an aid to a good meeting. Also, some participants (mainly fidgety guys) may need to move around quietly in the conference room as needed. Sitting too much can send brains into a zoned-out, bored rest state—particularly male brains. This can lead to side conversations and frustrating behavior that distracts the meeting, and may even degenerate into verbal snipes or dismissive gestures by men against women, or vice versa.

Skill 4: Return Meetings to Their Purpose

You as a leader need to keep the discussion or brainstorming focused; thus you have the right to return a meeting to its purpose. When you interrupt someone whose comments have become, in your opinion, tangential to the purpose, try this:

- If you are a man, interrupt with both a compliment and a permission request, such as "That's an interesting thought, but I'm going to pull us back to _____ ; is that okay?"
- If you are a woman, it is often more effective to simply say, "That's an interesting thought, but I'm going to pull us back to _____." Men often will answer a woman who asks, "Is that okay?" with a "No!" Women are less likely to do that. If you indeed want the meeting to move on to a new (or original) topic, you may need to refocus it with different male/female receptivity in mind.

Skill 5: Draw Out Talent

Leaders need to encourage participation from all attendees so that everyone's ability and talent comes to bear on the issue, design concept, or marketing strategy. Shy people often need to be called on—their brilliance may need to be brought out carefully. Overbearing and interrupting people may need to be taught better manners, by you!

- If you are a man trying to deal with an overbearing male, you might try, "Jim, what's up, man? You keep interrupting! Let people talk."
- If you are a woman trying to deal with an overbearing male, you might not get as much success with that approach—you might try, "We need to hear from everyone in the next five minutes if we're going to make our ending time. Let's hear now from people who haven't spoken."

Remember that women hear critical remarks from men differently than they do from women. Men hear critical remarks from women differently than they do from men. The issues we will discuss in the GenderTool on conflict resolution (Chapter Seven) are omnipresent for many men and women. They are part of our gender landscape. We do indeed need to develop different skills, at times, to deal effectively with overbearing women and men.

Skill 6: Care About Diversity

You may need to make the inclusion of diverse ideas and viewpoints a tacit action item in every meeting. Leaders and participants need to take a moment to consider whether diversity of opinion has been achieved before ending the meeting. You might ask yourself, "Did I get all gender opinions? Did I get every personality involved?" Every meeting that ends without gathering diversity of opinion is a meeting that has potentially lost ideas, talents, perspectives, and potential success items.

Skill 7: Channel Competitiveness

Some competitiveness between executives is a good thing, but too much is hurtful, especially when it's not a competition of ideas but rather a competition of personalities. Facilitate the meeting so team members' personalities work together, not against each other, even when their ideas may be in conflict with one another. Get mentoring and executive coaching as needed if you are seeing that your meetings have become driven by personality conflicts. Also see Chapter Seven for the GenderTool on conflict resolution.

Skill 8: Be Organized

Assign action items and next steps as you end meetings. Assign jobs to appropriate individuals. Being organized isn't just about printing out an agenda or having one displayed on the PowerPoint presentation. Organization is also about creating rituals for meetings, marking points, milestones, a kind of interactive rhythm that helps everyone proceed. Organization helps retain top talent, and organized meetings are frameworks that best make sure all voices get heard. If you are a notoriously bad organizer and you know someone who is a very good organizer, use that person's talent and give that person credit! Let that person help set up the meeting parameters, and thank him or her in front of others.

Skill 9: Be Open to the Post-Meeting Process

If you see that a person (woman or man) is dissatisfied with the meeting itself, take five minutes to debrief and hear the person's point of view after the meeting (or later that day). Leaders do make errors in meetings, missing what a woman or man really wants to say, rushing things, forgetting everything they have learned about running meetings. Because this happens, leaders need to invite other executives and employees to bring up, via e-mail or other channels, any serious issues that have been missed in the meeting.

Skill 10: Reach Out for Gender Help

Even after the meeting, take a little time to think about gender balance and gender intelligence. Ask yourself, "What did Sarah see in that meeting? What did Joe see in that meeting?" Get help before the next meeting, if needed—not only in skills development but also in filling in gaps in your own ability to read signals of all participants. Reach out to trusted people of the other gender for their assistance. You'll become all the wiser for it.

6

GenderTool 3

Improving Your Communication Skills
with Women and Men

The brain research on gender differences is very valuable with
respect to understanding differences in communication styles. Men
mean different things than women do, even if they are using the
same words. That causes misinterpretations. These misinterpretations can have an impact on the business and on people's careers.
It's very important that both men and women understand these
communication differences so they can work well together.

—JENNIFER ALLYN, MANAGING DIRECTOR, GENDER RETENTION
AND ADVANCEMENT, PRICEWATERHOUSECOOPERS

WHEN INEFFECTIVE COMMUNICATION GOES ON BETWEEN LEADERS, it can
carry over dangerously into all parts of your corporate culture. As emotional intelligence guru Daniel Goleman has pointed out, "Emotions
flow most strongly from the most powerful person in the room to others." Leaders have a profound and rewarding responsibility to acquire
the most gender-intelligent communication skills they can—*and* teach
them to others.

Here is a tool you can use immediately to improve your own communication as a leader and facilitate better communication in your
team and workplace between the genders.

Focusing on Verbal Communication

Be aware of and discuss the following five differences in language that exist between men and women who are trying to communicate what they need and want. As we help you work with each difference, we'll provide insights for men about women and for women about men, as well as tips you can use immediately to alter ineffective communication patterns.

Difference One

Women tend to use *more words* than men, relying greatly on verbal and written communication throughout the workday. Men use fewer words, in general, and will interrupt people (especially women) when they've reached what men consider their "word limit." (Of course, there are many reasons for interrupting, but this is a pervasive one).

Insight for Men About Women: By using lots of words, women stimulate many parts of the brain (both their own brains and their listeners') to see, feel, and sense possibly related ideas, experiences, and memories. This whole process can lead to ever-new design concepts and creative ways of accomplishing workplace goals.

However, women can tend to use so many words at one time that the person listening (often a man) will zone out, become distracted, interrupt (offending the woman), or become irritable. If you know a "wordy woman" (or man), help them notice the zoned-out look. If they see it in a lot of people, they'll have incentive to cut down on their words. Help them learn to give only essential information when that is all that is required.

Practical Strategy for Women: At the same time, if men are constantly interrupting you while you are giving essential information, point this out—make sure they know you feel disrespected. It is normal for any-one, woman or man, to interrupt someone who has gotten off point, but it destroys balanced leadership when interrupting behavior is not a strategy for workplace goals, but instead is a personal flaw in the listener or a signal of disrespect.

Insight for Women About Men: Using fewer words, men are forced to say what they mean more economically. This can be advantageous in tech fields. Also, the ability to interrupt and thereby secure the speaking turn or to make a point quickly can be advantageous in many work environments. However, men often think they have expressed what they meant or want when in fact their directions aren't clear and they have not provided enough examples or details for carry-through to be ensured.

Practical Strategy for Men: If you are such a man (or woman), concentrate on using one clear example for each instruction; for example, "I need _____ to happen, so I want you to do _____."

Difference Two

In their everyday conversations, women tend to *criticize themselves* more than men criticize themselves. Women often do this to match relationally with another person. ("Oh yes, I made that mistake, too.") Men tend to *criticize others* in order to match relationally. ("Look at that geek! He's not going anywhere in this company, you can tell.") Male leaders must be aware that in a professional environment women's self-criticism may not be verbalized and hence not visible. A woman who appears confident may still be beating herself up with self-criticism. This is one reason male leaders need to tailor their approach depending on the individual they are dealing with. A soft criticism—"You ought to have spent more time preparing for this client"—may be appropriate for a woman who is already self-critical, whereas for a male employee, a more blunt "Man, you blew that presentation" may be required to get the same effect.

Insight for Men About Women: Women tend to keep more bonds intact and help others feel better about themselves. This ability is often undervalued in the corporate world, yet it can in fact lead to increased productivity—people work harder when they feel good! However, a woman's humility will often be misunderstood as weakness.

Practical Strategy for Women: If you have experienced this, educate those around you that humility is not weakness.

Insight for Women About Men: Men tend to deflect negative feeling away from themselves. This is a good survival mechanism, but if you tend to take criticizing others too far, especially criticizing a friend, be wary of the day this catches up to you!

Practical Strategy for Men: Men will tend to miss their own mistakes, as focused as they are on others. A little self-deprecation might be in order, at least once a day.

If you are a very critical person, you might think about and express to a friend something you were wrong about today. It's a good exercise for stretching communication abilities in environments shared by women and men.

Difference Three

Men tend, more than women do, to direct word use toward the *success goal* they are focused on (in this area, men will sometimes use *more* words than women do). Women, as we've noted, will tend to use more words to manage the process by which success is gained.

Insight for Women About Men: Men may stay on a task more easily— especially moving as quickly as possible to the goal, unaware of and often unconcerned about any messes they leave along the way. They may often accomplish a singular goal more quickly than a female colleague would.

However, because they neglect to "process the process" as they go along, they may get to the goal and realize they haven't done it in a team, done it right, or even done it as effectively as they could have.

Practical Strategy for Men: If you have experienced this, slow down and talk out what you are doing!

Insight for Men About Women: Women tend to gravitate toward and excel in managerial positions that require a great deal of "processing the process." More and more of these kinds of jobs will be opening up over the coming decades.

However, women are sometimes disrespected by goal-oriented men for moving too slowly toward the goal (and spending too much time on the process).

Practical Strategy for Women: If you use a lot of words related to process, focus on finding a middle ground between process and product. Get advice from others about how to find this middle ground in your particular environment—and obviously, make sure the friends you get advice from are trustworthy allies.

Difference Four

Men tend to spend more verbal time showing their own *accomplishments and prowess* than women do. Women tend to spend less time this way, instead spending more time asking *questions,* like "What did you say?" "What did you mean?" and "So, what did you do?" which specifically de-emphasize their own prowess in favor of hearing another's accomplishments.

Insight for Women About Men: Men who talk about their accomplishments tend to get more notice than others do, especially shyer women. However, people tend not to want to work with or for them, as they are tired of hearing about their individual accomplishments ("What a narcissist!").

Practical Strategy for Men: If you spend a lot of time talking about yourself in the workplace, be aware that some men and more women are probably wondering about ways they can spend less time working for and with you.

Insight for Men About Women: Women will often be the sought-after person for a conversation or when another person is looking for psychosocial support.

However, women may spend so much time in this kind of interaction that they neglect to position themselves competitively in the workplace.

Practical Strategy for Women: If you constantly go out of your way to ask how others are feeling, try to become aware of this and spend a little more time making sure a few key people hear your accomplishments.

Difference Five

Women tend to spend more verbal time on individual *emotion memories* and individual family and relational memories than men. Men tend to spend more words on trivia and outcomes of *large social aggression-based groupings* (such as sports, factual history), and on showing dominance (one-upmanship).

Insight for Men About Women: Women tend to experience a richer emotion-filled life, enjoying the neural "hits" of emotion and feeling from satisfying memories and emotional connections.

However, they often find themselves unable to connect with men (especially men at the top) who are so competitive and aggressive by nature that they don't even try to have this conversation.

Practical Strategy for Women: If you are a woman climbing a corporate hierarchy, you may well need to talk in a more bottom-line, factual way with men.

Insights for Women About Men: Dealing with less emotion every day quite often makes task focus easier. Those who are focused on a software development task, for instance, may not need to experience much emotion at all in a day (except the excitement of reaching a goal).

However, those who are less emotional may miss a lot! When they get hurt emotionally, they lack the language to deal with the hurt. Sometimes they turn this energy into addictions or other negative behavior.

Practical Strategy for Men: If you are unable to connect with others verbally except through very limited conversations, you may need to connect with a mentor—female or male—who can help you develop more emotional literacy. Your health could depend on it, as could your job.

Burning Question: How Much Do You Have to Change Your Communication Style?

The verbal differences and action tips just presented beg the question most often asked about gender intelligence: How much do I have to change my communication style to become more effective in the workplace? And for leaders, how much change is necessary in order to become the best leader possible?

In the past, our workplaces cut women off from power because of a superficial sense of gender; more recently, we have attributed communication differences to socialization and thus pretended they would disappear within a generation if we just retrained everyone to be androgynous communicators.

Now, fortunately, with leaders like you gaining a fundamental understanding of the hard-wired differences in verbal communication styles, we can alter individual misinterpretations through understanding and take action to maximize each gender's potential. And as Mother Teresa said, "Understanding means there is nothing to forgive."

Here is a quick checklist that will help you focus on the new understanding and new action of accepting gender differences in verbal styles as corporate assets.

To-Do Checklist—For Executives and Managers

❑ Be open to altering communication skills in order to be more effective with any important population, specifically women and men. Follow this openness with immediate gender education and training. Learn what the other gender is thinking, how the other gender communicates, what makes the other gender tick. Listen more carefully to her than you used to. When he talks, watch his body language more attentively than you used to.

❑ Follow education and observation with your own trust of your newly sharpened instincts. Let your natural adaptive mechanisms operate as you follow up education with *action*. Trust that you, whether man or woman, have a lot of good intuition about how to be effective—intuition that may need deeper gender education to make it fully active and gender intelligent.

❑ Learn the specific communication pitfalls you and your team members need to work on. You don't have to change who you are—you can't!—but you can change what you say and how you say it, once you know what the men and women in your team need from you, and you from them.

❑ Go beyond stereotypes about the other gender (or your own) and move into a science-based approach to biological trends in communication.

If you follow these steps, you'll come to a place of verbal communication in which you'll experience less gender tension and enjoy more sense of humor; less "he's out to get me" and more "I know how to handle him"; less "she's incompetent and insecure" and more "I missed what she's trying to say until now."

Your personality won't change, however; nor will you change the personalities of the people you work with.

Success in leadership and relationships in the workplace is not measured by creating a staid environment in which every man and woman communicates in exactly the same industrial way—having changed or been remolded to accommodate some sort of communication style that, like an industrial product, is presumed will work for everyone. Rather, success in gender relations among leaders (as in long-term marriage) is best measured by respect among women and men for one another's capabilities, specifically in the case of this verbal tool: their words. We don't generally need to change who we are to reap the benefits of this mutual respect. But the corporate culture we exist in may indeed need to change from both the traditionalist and feminist models regarding what should and should not be said (and done) in the workplace.

Focusing on Nonverbal Communication

In looking at verbal communication differences, we suggested some awareness and action tips that can help you as an individual become more effective with the other gender. In a similar vein, let's look now at nonverbal communication. Here are some differences you may need to navigate every day at work.

??? Did You Know ???

Women Tend To . . .

- Women tend to communicate with their facial expressions, using more variety than men, especially to show approval (which in turn keeps social cohesion secure). For instance, they nod when someone is speaking more than men do. Keep in mind that their nodding does not necessarily mean agreement; it may only mean "Yes, I hear you."
- Women tend to hold more eye contact during everyday conversation, whereas men tend to stand more "shoulder to shoulder." Exceptions are conflict situations: in these, men tend to hold more eye contact than women, using eye contact as a territory marker and aggression tool; women (and shy men) tend to lower their eyes in high-stress situations.
- Women tend to smile when listening, while men tend to squint and frown more.
- Women tend to be good at reading social cues, but some women (and some men) can tend to *overread* social cues, reading more into them than may be there. The highly active cingulate gyrus we discussed in Chapter Two is a possible reason for this.
- Women tend to *use less physical space* while communicating, whereas men tend to spread their legs out more, gesture their arms more widely, move around in more physical space.

Men Tend To . . .

- Men tend to believe more than women do that their *nonverbal relational cues* are being picked up.
- Men tend to notice fewer nonverbal cues of emotion, whether *on faces or in physical gestures,* than women do.

- Men also often *misread women's facial expressions* of frustration or annoyance—leading women to think that men don't care.
- When men are most efficient in reading cues, it tends to be in the area of *physical aggression.*
- Men tend to *express their anger* more nonverbally (and physically) than women do, and more quickly expel the anger through physical bursts of energy, such as hitting a table.
- Men often listen without as much facial attentiveness as women exhibit. Women can tend to feel not heard by men who recline away from them or listen with a blank face.

If you are a woman speaking at a meeting to a mix of women and men, you may notice differences in nonverbal cues, especially between women and men. While you are speaking, you may notice that the women appear to be more receptive to what you are saying than the men. Maybe they are—or maybe the men just aren't showing their receptivity the way the women are. To ascertain what the men really think, you may need to ask them.

Communication Differences in Sales

Training a sales force is a fundamental area of business leadership and management. Sales is greatly impacted by the gender differences—after all, sales is *all* about communication with men and women.

When we think about the fundamental brain differences between men and women, we can also see those differences manifested in their speech patterns during sales. Men often communicate in sales situations by being data- and product-directed: they may interrupt, they use less emotion, they stay more on topic and don't get personal (of course there are exceptions to this), and they tend to make declarative statements about a product.

Women, on the other hand, tend to be more wired to cross-connect and build relationships when they sell; therefore, their speech tends to be geared toward being inclusive and more relational; they ask more questions, they try to get to know the person on a personal level, and they use tag endings ("It's a nice day, isn't it?") that compel the other person to communicate back.

Often managers will ask, "So, who is better in sales, men or women?" Neither is better biologically—they are different!

Try This
Selling to Men

Aware that a lot of selling/marketing research about gender addresses how to market and sell to women (see, for example, the books *The Power of the Purse* and *Selling to Women*), speaker and trainer Karen Purves (see Notes and Resources) completed a long-term research project to see how brain-based gender differences affect sales to men. She then developed a twelve-point program that combined this gender/brain research with field research.

Karen shared three of her communication insights and tools with us.

First, I found that it is most effective to ask a man what he *thinks* about something, or what he *thinks* is a good next step. This is as opposed to "What do you want to *do* next?" When I've helped sales forces apply this in the field, I often get back follow-up comments like, "This really works: it takes pressure off the guy, increases his comfort, and increases his likelihood to buy from me."

Second, when men sometimes act impulsively in business buying decisions, salespeople should use this to their advantage. Soft close early if he's ready. It saves time, effort and money. The idea here isn't that *all* men are impulsive—the success idea here is to check to see if *this* man is ready to buy with very little information or time invested.

Third, *competition* really works when selling to men (not all, but many). Whether it is through quotas or competing bids, almost every industry has or can include competitive elements. When you convey information about competition, most men prefer you to state the information in facts and figures, as opposed to stories.

If you as a leader are responsible for a sales force, here are a number of communication differences you will want to look at closely as you add brain-based gender differences to your assessment of the talents you are managing. Use these to help your sales team alter their techniques to fit the women or men they are selling to.

- Men tend to speak in louder voices than women do. They also tend to use loudness to emphasize points. If you see it in the males in your sales force, make sure it fits the product and customer.
- Given that men tend to interrupt more than women, they (and similar women) often need help, especially if they are going to sell to women, in listening better—and not interrupting too often.
- Women talk more about themselves, revealing more about their lives than men do. Is this a good fit for your product? It might well be. But it might not be, especially if the woman is going to sell to a man who really doesn't care a lot about the person he is buying from.
- Men more directly accuse—"You didn't fill that order." Women are more likely to ask, "Why didn't you fill that order?" Generally, both kinds of communication can be useful in different situations. If you see someone in your sales force overemphasizing either way of communicating, you may need to mentor them toward a middle ground.

- Women tend to include more pleasant endings, such as "Have a nice day." They use lots of questions, and they use upward inflections, making statements into questions through inflection. "It's a nice day, isn't it?" Men tend to ask fewer questions to stimulate conversation with customers than women do. Men tend to end sentences in more abrupt ways, including their phone conversations. Men also tend to avoid upward inflections. Be very clear on when and where and with whom each of these strategies works.

Your sales force may need your men to "peer mentor" your women, and vice versa. Given that selling takes place with both women and men, all the skills are needed.

Ultimately, in general, if a man is selling to a woman, he may need to stretch his emotional abilities to try to build a relationship, not just get to the bottom line of the sale.

Similarly, in general, if a woman is selling to a man, she may need to be cognizant that men often don't like talking a lot about their personal lives or beating around the bush. Often, they just want you to get to the bottom line using as few words as possible.

GenderTool 4

*Improving Your Conflict Resolution Skills
with Men and Women*

Effective conflict skills are crucial emotional literacy skills, and they
are crucial to the contemporary workplace.

—DANIEL GOLEMAN, AUTHOR, *EMOTIONAL INTELLIGENCE*
AND SOCIAL INTELLIGENCE

IN CORPORATIONS, MEN AND WOMEN WORK TOGETHER for eight to ten or
more hours a day. They are like an extended family. This is never more
apparent than when there is conflict. Just as a marriage can end in
divorce because of deeply rooted conflicts, work teams can be made or
broken by their ability or inability to handle conflicts together.

As we move through this tool, please remember that conflict is inevi-
table in relationships, and if done well, it is a *good* thing. It increases
bonding and leads to creativity and new thinking. We don't want to try to
remove conflict from relationships. We want to do conflict well, because
when done *badly,* it can be dangerous to a team and a corporate culture.

Focusing on Conflict

Men and women involved in a conflict tend to find their emotions
escalating along a continuum from triggered to angry. All of us can
experience this continuum, and each step in the continuum provides

opportunity to use conflict resolution skills. The following statements express the experience of moving along that continuum; the "I" can be either gender, with men and women experiencing each in their own way:

- *Triggered:* Something happens or is said that stimulates a stress emotion in me.
- *Irritated:* I feel my heart beating harder; my mind is focused, attentive, wary—and it's now directed at someone or something.
- *Annoyed:* The internal feelings have gone on for more than a few moments—they are building, and I may be getting ready to respond defensively or offensively.
- *Angry:* My eyes, face, body, voice may now become physically and obviously responsive to the person or situation that angered me.

Noticing Differences Between Women and Men in Conflict

- Men tend to become more physically dominant during conflict.
- Men tend to curse more—especially with men—and women less (cursing is a dominance/territoriality strategy during conflict).
- There are more connections to the emotional centers in female brains, so women are more likely to feel conflict more and worry about how it is somehow their fault than to think about how to solve it immediately.
- Men often distance themselves from conflict, typically deciding the problem is external to them and they don't need to deal with it.
- Women often personalize conflicts for longer periods of time than men do, and they store up anger and discomfort that can lead, in the long term, to loss of the woman and her talent from the team.
- For men, a primary mistake in angry conflicts is not returning to the issues of the conflict and resolving them (even later, after the fury is gone). Men will often think the conflict has been resolved because it is finished inside them. They won't realize how hurt the woman feels; they won't value her feelings. This is dangerous

to corporate culture—it can lead in the long term to women leaving this particular workplace and taking their talent elsewhere.

- For women, a primary mistake is saying to men right in the middle of the conflict situation, "What's happening? What are you feeling? Talk to me." When the male brain becomes angry, the swelling of the amygdala in the limbic system often leads to a near closure of a lot of the man's verbal circuits. Whereas amygdalic swelling in the female brain can open up a lot of her words and thoughts, so she may want to "talk it out right now to seek understanding" as the key to resolution, the man's angry brain response may require that he delay verbal reaction, walk away, and return several minutes later.

As you are looking at how you (and the women and men around you) move through the conflict emotion continuum, it is crucial to follow up this information about the male and female brain by busting a contemporary myth in your team: good conflict is not achieved through *one* verbal style of conflict resolution. There are many good approaches, and some don't involve talking a lot.

Over the last twenty years, our culture has developed a love of words for resolving conflict ("Talk to me," "Tell me what you're feeling"). That is wonderful, but it is not necessarily the best way to handle every situation. "Tell me what you're feeling" can create angry outbursts and escalate the conflict. As you look at conflicts that may lead to anger in your team, open yourself and others up to a *number* of methods to de-escalate the conflict:

To-Do Checklist—Dealing with Anger

- ❑ *Relax ASAP:* Do what you have to do to cut back on your stress levels. This may include turning away with a statement like, "I'll get back to you on this in five minutes," then doing some deep breathing, listening to music, or doing another activity, like scanning through your e-mail, to get your mind onto something else.
- ❑ *Experience, Express, Expel:* Let your emotions move through their natural cycle in a safe way. This means feeling the anger,

expressing it (even physically, in physical exercise or a safe, physical burst of energy), and expelling it by breathing it out, or getting it out of your system via a conversation with a friend. Develop a personal practice for these three Es. You may accomplish this differently than the man or woman you are in conflict with.

❑ *If You Walk Away, Return:* If you need to walk away to distract yourself from the stress and defuse the situation, make sure to find a way to return to the other person when the stress is lower. Complete the conversation. If you don't do this, you have abandoned the other person to a state of vulnerability that you are partially responsible for. There are generally unforeseen and disturbing consequences to this kind of emotional and social abandonment.

❑ *Examine Your Thoughts:* Examine your own thoughts, then discuss with your team how quickly you and others around you escalate the feelings on the conflict continuum. If you get triggered easily (often overreacting to small stuff) or if you often escalate quickly, you may need coaching or mentoring, or other similar assistance.

As you discuss all these elements, if you know particular people who escalate too quickly and unreasonably, get coaching for them. They may need your help and the help of mentors and coaches to specifically alter these approaches to their own emotions.

Try This
Examine Approaches That Escalate Conflict

Here are five approaches to conflict that can make conflict worse. These are valuable discussion tools. It can be helpful to you and your team to look carefully at them. As we provide them here, the "I" in the statements that articulate them can be of either gender, though you may intuitively notice differences in how they appear in men and women around you.

Self-superiority

Most of the "conflicts" at work seem trivial to me or beneath me. I figure, "Let someone else solve that." If you know a leader who uses this kind of approach, mentor him or her as soon as possible. If this leader is the CEO, finding just the right mentor will not be easy, but perhaps a directive and strong executive coach can help.

The best defense is a good offense

When I sense someone moving toward conflict, I sense dominance, manipulation, control, or even abandonment. This unconsciously triggers a counterattack—I do something that escalates the conflict, either behind the person's back or right in the person's face. If this "I" is you, count to ten and hold back on offense as long as possible. Over time, you may notice other possibilities for relationship filling up the time and space you formerly devoted to offense and attack.

Making universal statements

I use "always," "never," and other distancing words in communications, such as "Joe never delivers within budget." This is a trap men and women can fall into that escalates conflict. It almost always brings on a counter, "No I'm not," or "You're full of it" kind of internal dialogue, even if the words are not spoken aloud.

A too-long memory

I have a good memory for emotional history, and I use this to bring up past failures, inadequacies, and mistakes another person has made. This is a dominance mechanism I practice to make sure the other party knows who is boss. If you use this method too much, you are pushing away allies. During a conflict, work hard to stay focused on the problem at hand, rather than the long history of a relationship.

Triangulation

When I'm upset I like to go to a colleague to talk it out ("You wouldn't believe what Jim did"), but sometimes my colleague will pass along my complaint to the person I'm angry with ("Mary's really upset with you") or to the rest of the team, which only makes things worse. Gossip is gossip, pure and simple. If we are talking about someone behind his or her back, everyone is generally the loser. If you tend toward this strategy, get help in curtailing the behavior. Take immediate responsibility for it! It is dangerous to a team's cohesion and to your own corporate future.

Try This
Focus on Pushing Through Cultural Differences in Gender

We did executive coaching for a female leader at a gas company who was having problems with one of her direct reports. He came from a country in which he had never had to work with women, much less work under a female boss. Among the difficulties this situation created was his penchant for regularly bypassing her to talk with her male boss about team issues. When she confronted him on this inappropriate behavior, he became uncomfortable, avoided eye contact, and changed the subject. The conflict between these two individuals escalated painfully for the whole company.

Tradition and culture are a source of conflict between women and men. More and more men from traditionalist countries are adapting to female bosses than was the case thirty years ago; at the same time, more and more men and women are entering the workforce from traditionalist countries. Many not only are confused by the Western transition from patriarchal to feminist frames, but also are completely misinterpreting female behaviors as inferior. When the tradition of male dominance is overlaid on all of this, there can be significant culture-based conflicts between men and women.

Gender intelligence training and coaching becomes crucial in this situation. Traditionalist men and women cannot erase how they were raised, but they can be just as engaged as anyone else by how neutrally different men and women are. As they join everyone around them in gaining gender intelligence, they often find a commonality with coworkers, as understanding the other gender becomes a common topic of discussion.

Beyond this training and coaching, it is crucial that male bosses unite with female bosses to confront and reorient the traditionalist male employee to accept the authority of the woman. It can take many months, but it can remove many more months of conflict. Often, men simply need other men to tell them what they must do with respect to women's unique gifts and authority.

Authentic leadership is about taking responsibility for one's actions. Our only real authority as individuals on a leadership team comes from that authentic act. We can't control others, but we can control ourselves. This holds especially true when we are navigating conflicts between ourselves and the other gender.

The following situational exercise can help you direct yourself toward full authenticity in conflicts with anyone, especially the other gender. You can complete this exercise in your team meeting or alone.

Ultimately, as you ponder the questions in the exercise (and they can take a few days to really process), you are identifying a crucial element of all conflict, especially male/female leadership conflict: the *blame frame*. In the blame frame, our focus remains on blaming the other gender and

Situational Exercise

Recall a situation in which you faced a conflict with a person of the other gender—think of one in particular that wasn't resolved to your satisfaction. Invest a few minutes in thinking through the following:

- What happened with the other person?
- How did I feel?
- What did I say or do in reaction to those feelings?
- Who did I talk to, including the other person and any others?
- How was the situation resolved?

Once you've thought back, even taken some notes, check whether any of the following questions applied to this conflict:

- ❏ Did I immediately think the other person was all wrong?
- ❏ Did I spend a lot of time arguing about who was right or wrong?
- ❏ Did I keep experiencing anger (even shock) when my point wasn't accepted by the other person?
- ❏ Did the other person actively blame me, in words or deeds, or did I just feel blamed?
- ❏ Did I gossip with someone else about the conflict and the other person?
- ❏ Did I keep mulling it over, even when the other person thought the conflict was over? If so, did I gain anything by this constant processing?
- ❏ If I got defensive at the beginning of the conflict (which is pretty normal for all of us), how quickly was I able to move toward resolution of the conflict? Did the other person's gender affect how quickly or slowly I got defensive or resolved the conflict?

❑ Did I feel victimized, wrongly accused, misunderstood, or misinterpreted? Why? How did my gender and the gender of the other person affect these feelings?

❑ Do I feel committed to a relationship with this other person right now? If so, are there remaining issues in the conflict that we need to talk about?

❑ Am I in a win-win situation now (involving compromise by both of us) with the other person?

the person of the other gender. We hope that this book and this exercise help you move toward an *outcome frame* with this other person. In the outcome frame, your focus is not on the history of the conflict or blame, but on finding a solution. Here are the blame frame and outcome frame in a nutshell.

BLAME FRAME	OUTCOME FRAME
Seeks compliance	Solution-oriented
You or me	You *and* me
Right or wrong	Win-win
Attached to opinion	Unattached to opinion
Reactive	Reflective
Finding fault	Zero judgment
Gossip	Takes responsibility

It is natural to occupy the blame frame at times, especially when working with the other gender. Gender intelligence includes a strong dose of moving as an individual and a team toward outcome frames. This movement is quite liberating. Balanced leadership between women and men often depends on it.

In the next chapter, as we look carefully at the issue of retention and advancement of women, we carry forward all four GenderTools and their strategies and insights. Use of these tools can play a critical role in enabling the retention and advancement of women, and the success-oriented, profitable, and very powerful gender balance it leads to.

In the end, this critical process takes place when leaders are conscious, not only of brain and cultural differences, but also of how to negotiate, meet, relate, communicate, and engage in conflict together, in the long haul.

PART

The Applications

Ensuring Gender-Balanced Leadership in the Long Term

There are lots of times, of course, when men and women have to be relatively androgynous in their leadership goals and capabilities—they each have to do what the other does. But there are also many times when a man or a woman is just better suited for the immediate "moment" the executive team is facing.

Tapping into these different assets has been proven to work in a number of companies—income growth, workplace productivity, and team cohesion improve. The companies make more money. Men and women don't lead the same way, and a corporation needs both assets, especially as the world economy goes global.

—MITTIE PEDRAZA, CORPORATE ATTORNEY

8

Helping Women
Retaining, Motivating, and Working with Female Talent

We are heading for a perfect storm in the labor market. There is reduced supply coming into the labor market, increased numbers of baby boomers leaving the market, and at the same time, an increasing demand for talent as the economy grows. In all this, women are the largest new talent pool. If we don't retain and advance their talent, we will not fully succeed.

—SEAN MCCONKEY, DELOITTE & TOUCHE

A CEO OF AN ELECTRONICS COMPANY RECENTLY TOLD US, "I know there's something going on when eight out of ten people on my executive team are men. I know we are missing out on intelligence, innovation, and insight that women would bring. We're profitable now, but we could be more profitable if we understood how to bring women's gifts and insights to the leadership table."

He is just one of the executives who know that in the general marketplace, 83 percent of consumer spending is done by women. And in his business in particular—electronics—51 percent of the customers are women, *and* women influence 89 percent of all consumer electronic purchase decisions.

This CEO is exemplary of the men and women we meet running companies—they are leaders like you who sense or know outright the importance of understanding and equally valuing women's needs, perceptions, buying power, and leadership skills. As we continue through the new millennium, the issue faced by these executives and companies is not whether or not to include women, but how to tap women's capabilities to make a company more competitive and valuable in both human and financial terms.

The insights from brain research in the first chapters of this book have, we hope, helped you be more gender intelligent—interested in and clear about who the people around you are, what makes them tick, and what unique gender talents they possess. In Part One, we aimed to help you discuss in your leadership teams how to guide your corporation toward greater use of all your brain-based assets—both female and male. In Part Two, we introduced GenderTools designed to help you immediately put your new gender intelligence to work on a day-to-day basis so that wisdom could immediately be put into practice.

Now, in Part Three, we will help you apply what you have learned to the development of gender balance in your corporation's hierarchy. We will explore with you key obstacles you may face as your corporation tries to develop gender balance, and practical ways to remove those obstacles. You will learn about how other corporations like yours have used the information and tools of gender intelligence to create gender balance and increase market share and profitability. You'll also gain access to further tools, analysis, and innovations to help you inculcate gender balance into your corporation's structure well into the future.

Let's begin this application process by noting that when corporations solve gender issues through application of brain-based gender difference research, they improve their bottom line. In clear financial terms, they become more profitable when they pay attention to gender balance. And as you'll learn in this chapter on women's talents, when corporations make full use of female talent, they discover new avenues for revenue and growth.

Success Stories: How Gender-Balanced Leadership Improves the Bottom Line

Catalyst Corporation has found that "the group of companies with the highest representation of women on their top management teams experienced better financial performance than the group of companies with the lowest women's representation. This finding holds for both financial measures analyzed: Return on Equity (ROE), which is 35.1 percent higher, and Total Return to Shareholders (TRS), which is 34.0 percent higher."

A number of companies we've worked with have specifically proven Catalyst's conclusions. These companies brought gender intelligence training into their corporate culture because, like the CEO we mentioned at the outset of this chapter, they saw how much female talent they were undervaluing, not using, or outright losing. They realized that the loss of talent led to a loss of revenue and value. Their efforts to alter their situation were rewarded by a dramatically improved bottom line.

Let's look at two of the companies we've worked with specifically: one, IBM, in the technological sector, the other, Deloitte & Touche, in finance.

Innovations in the Technology Sector: Featuring IBM

IBM is a technology company that decided to become gender intelligent and balanced. When Lou Gerstner became CEO of IBM, he instituted a task force charged with (1) discovering and defining the gender and racial differences among various constituent groups of personnel in the corporation, and (2) finding ways to appeal to a broader spectrum of these managers and employees so that IBM could not only become the most productive workplace possible for all its constituent groups, but also appeal in the long term to the broadest possible group of diverse customers worldwide. Specifically in the area of gender, the IBM diversity task force discovered wide gaps in male/female representation and a severe loss of female talent.

Barbara was first called in by IBM Canada in 1992. The company's internal research had identified a significant gender gap: at progressively more senior levels there were correspondingly fewer women. Their turnover among women in the sales function came at enormous cost and was a blow to their attempt to build talent. They took a sociological stance on the problem initially—ending up, for a time, wondering if they were only facing the issue of women leaving to have children. Barbara and her team were able to help IBM recognize that one of the things that mattered most was underlying brain differences between women and men. Women's ways of being, working, and leading were not understood or valued at IBM. Women did not feel needed.

For instance, men in the company would see a woman negotiating differently and perceive that the woman lacked negotiation skills. Women, on the other hand, would see men pushing to get a decision without talking about the context and valuing women's opinions, and they would conclude that the men were dismissing their input.

A constant stream of misinterpretations, based on differences in how men and women perceive and act in the workplace, were a core problem, and IBM decided to deal with it head-on. The company ran a series of workshops to transform the mind-set of their managers. Men and women came to see brain-based gender differences not as a hindrance or something to be accommodated, but as an advantage the team could use.

Through this process—which began as a two-year training program—the misconceptions and assumptions that had been driving men and women apart were gradually removed. Over the two-year period, *turnover of women professionals in sales was greatly reduced.* Not only did this work address the problem of retaining female talent, but it was also great for the company's reputation. IBM was recognized in *Working Mother* magazine and received a number of accolades and awards. Most important, IBM's focus on creating a woman-friendly environment helped them make money.

As Ted Childs, vice president of Global Diversity Workforce at IBM, recently said, "Our women executive appointments worldwide over the last nine years are up 425 percent." Maria Ferris, director of

IBM's Workforce Diversity Programs, corroborated these gains: "In 2005, IBM attained a significant milestone—1,000 women executives globally (versus only 185 in 1995)." As Childs and Ferris have pointed out, this advancement was a significant reason for bottom-line gains in areas in which diversity is key, such as the growth in the company's small and medium-sized business sales and marketing sector—from $10 million in 1998 to more than $100 million in 2003. To absorb information about gender balance and apply it throughout the corporation, IBM made a number of structural and functional changes.

Try This
What IBM Did

Structural changes at IBM, which can be made at any company, included the following:

- IBM developed a task force to study gender balance issues and incorporated gender awareness training (such as depicted in this book) into various management levels.
- Executives were asked to reach out personally to constituent employee groups, asking them to partner with the company in addressing the gender balance challenge.
- IBM created a substantial mentoring system in which executives specifically mentored individuals and groups in career advancement and work/life balance (see Chapter Ten for practical strategies for setting up your own corporation's gender mentoring and coaching system).
- IBM instituted a new policy whereby "managing diversity" become one of the core competencies used to assess managers' performance. Managers were required to focus on gender balance.
- Leaders were called on to act as role models and mentors, including leaders who were juggling motherhood and work/ life balance—two key issues for retention of women.

Innovations in the Financial Sector: Featuring Deloitte & Touche

When Barbara began working with Deloitte & Touche, they had been doing a great job of attracting talent—for instance, they were heavily recruiting for women in universities and succeeding in getting talented women to join the firm—but they couldn't retain the women in whom they were investing value and money in training. Deloitte & Touche felt that they had become a kind of a university for women, providing great development only to see the women get fed up and leave for a competitor. They were losing millions of dollars in this way.

Managing partner Yezdi Pavri recalls, "We studied the issues facing female professionals and found they didn't feel as included and valued as men. We had lots of data to reflect this. For instance, our women were not progressing to the senior ranks in our firm, and our surveys showed that women did not feel valued, and they didn't have as great an opportunity to advance in the firm as men did. This loss of talented people hampered our ability to grow our business in the medium and long term."

As Deloitte & Touche's leadership teams began to engage in training to build awareness of brain-based gender differences, they came to see that simply focusing on hiring lots of women at the entry level wouldn't solve the retention issue. Talented women needed the company to deal with fundamental differences in how men and women behave and think, and to take advantage of those differences. Women were leaving this financial powerhouse because, for instance, when some male senior partners got ready to decide who to put into a senior role, they were not as attuned as they needed to be to the potential of women, and they couldn't recognize the differences in how women solve problems, or lead teams, or approach a situation—differences that are strengths. Even though women were getting results, the men just didn't feel comfortable with how women were getting those results, so they didn't advance the women, and the women finally left.

Furthermore, leaders at Deloitte & Touche discovered that some women who did get promoted felt obliged to take on a male persona, to force their natural strengths into the unnatural mode of the male brain—the third sex phenomenon. Even among the women who could do this, many didn't want to, and many who did do it found it a strain; they could not be their authentic selves at work. Many of them started showing signals of dissatisfaction, and then within a year or two (sometimes sooner) were gone.

The hard work done at Deloitte & Touche (and at IBM and many of the other companies acknowledged at the beginning of this book) has been revolutionary for the development of gender intelligence in the workplace. Executives at Deloitte & Touche not only cared about gender balance but also saw the wisdom of going right to the fundamentals of understanding and training in brain-based gender differences. They looked beyond the purely traditionalist and purely feminist frame to take in new scientific information.

Ultimately, straightforward and powerful solutions emerged. As Yezdi Pavri recently told us, "At first, we didn't recognize differences in how women solve problems, lead teams, or approach situations, but that has changed. Now we have made tremendous progress reshaping our culture. We have reduced our turnover rate dramatically. We have increased our representation of women at senior levels. We have provided training on understanding the strengths in gender differences; we have done this for partners, managers, and staff. This equipped our professionals with the knowledge and skills they need to create an inclusive environment. The results speak for themselves."

Deloitte & Touche is now a firm that does not try to change women into men (or men into women), but focuses primarily on changing mindsets so that managers recognized how the brain differences manifest themselves in the workplace. This removes blind spots and obstacles. As partners learn that men and women are fundamentally wired differently, it gives them new insight into how they should coach women, how they should understand women, and which women they should promote.

The business outcomes have been important for the firm. Before the initiative to train partners about brain differences, only 16 percent of women felt they had an equal chance of getting ahead (a problem men were largely blind to, with 66 percent of men feeling the chances for women were equal). After the initiative, 62 percent of women felt they had an equal chance. This perception was immediately linked to retention and thus to bottom-line numbers. *Deloitte & Touche–USA estimates it is saving $190 million a year through reduced turnover.*

What Women Want? No, What Women Need!

The organizations we've featured show how important gender balance can be to corporate success. These companies have come to understand *what women need* in order to feel a part of the corporation's leadership, and thus to be retained and advance—and ultimately, to share their gifts, and their methods of success, with the corporation's bottom line.

Let's explore what women in these and other companies have said they need in order to feel fulfilled in a corporation and, most important, to apply their talents in the corporation's leadership. The information you read in this section is based on our study of over two thousand workshops and corporate initiatives over the last twenty years. As we work with a company, the leaders provide information to us via diagnostic tools that we are able to summarize and use in training. Through this information, we are able to understand why women stay at a particular corporation and why they leave—their reasons are generally linked to their getting satisfaction not in what they *want*, but in what they *need*.

??? Did You Know ???

What Women Need?

In our study of what women need in order to be retained and advance, these were the most common responses:

- Women need work/life flexibility (men need this, too, as we'll explore in the next chapter).
- Women need men to understand that women's and men's needs are not separate, but interdependent.
- Women need to be respected for who they are—they are not men.

- Women need to be validated with more verbal encouragement than managers and coworkers may realize.
- Women need to be mentored in a gender-intelligent way.
- Women need to be mentored toward promotion, especially in male-dominant environments in which men are more likely to be promoted just because they are men.
- Women need businesses to understand that meeting women's needs can increase the bottom line.
- Women need women to support them; in particular, younger women need older women to support and empower them.
- Women need to be more strategic and proactive in expressing their career expectations.
- Women need men to be educated on how to best communicate with them, and they need to gain education in how best to communicate with men.

As women leave high-level positions at corporations, the corporate culture often believes the women leave to start families (the familiar accusation is "women want to have it all—have families and to be at the top of the corporation—but they won't put in the hours at work, so they just give in and go have families"). Corporations used to think this way (and some still do), but our study shows this to be only partially true. Many women say they are leaving a corporation to have a family, but soon turn up at a different, more woman-friendly company. A recent Catalyst Corporation study corroborated this finding, showing that while some women certainly leave the corporate world to have their families, most actually walk out of one corporation into another one that better fits their *needs* as executives, managers, and women.

This is quite logical, of course, and it can be said of men, too. Men have needs—when those natural needs are met, they do a better job. When those needs are not met, they will seek other opportunities (we will look closely at men's needs in the next chapter).

When women's needs are not met, what *signals* do they send out to a corporation? The corporation's leadership team needs to read these signals and act on them quickly.

Try This
Read Women's Signals of Unmet Needs

When a woman's needs are not met by the leadership team, you should be able to see some of these signals:

- She may tell a confidante or mentor that she feels devalued.
- She may try to assert her unique approach to a corporate issue, but have it shot down so many times that she finally stops asserting (and begins planning her exit strategy).
- She may begin to isolate herself from the corporation or team, feeling a disconnect between her leadership style and her colleagues.
- She may disconnect emotionally—talk less to others, express herself less, relate less.
- She may stop risk taking—in issues of product design, relationships, corporate functioning (preparing herself to move elsewhere, and saving her energy for the new job).
- She may seem to lose her sense of personal motivation to succeed beyond expectations. Her work may seem to become mediocre when in fact she may be capable of the highest level of work (just not here, at this corporation).
- She may begin to complain to confidantes more than she did before; for example, people may say, "She's changed; she's become a whiner," not realizing she is trying to get her needs met, without success.

If you are seeing these sorts of signals from a female leader you value, it is important to meet with her as soon as possible to try to understand what her needs are and how the mismatch between the leadership culture and her nature and needs can be resolved.

IBM, Deloitte & Touche, and many other corporations have invested in an evolutionary perspective—that women's needs can be met and that balanced leadership is not only fair but can bring good financial results. This perspective holds true not only within leadership teams, but also between leadership teams and client leaders.

John Maxwell, a senior partner at PricewaterhouseCoopers, gave us this anecdotal example of what we mean:

> We were working with one company whose treasurer was a woman. I learned that she wasn't happy; we were poised to lose her company's account. I went in to see her and value her perspective, and she could tell I wanted to know what was wrong, what she needed. It was terrific; she really opened up, expressed what she was feeling, and actually cried. The way the emotion was expressed was different from what you would find in a man, but luckily I knew how to deal with that. And actually, her way of expressing herself was refreshing. I could get to the root of the problem quickly. She told me she had felt that our male consultant hadn't been treating her as if she was as capable as she really was. Once I knew that, we were able to correct our approach.

As this kind of woman-friendly thinking is becoming a strength area for corporations, the reach of positive results is spreading. Even in the beleaguered airline industry, a recent example of direct positive results from meeting women's needs became clear. Pete McDonald, chief operating officer of United Airlines (UAL), learned about powerful gender differences and made a concerted effort to make sure female leaders advanced in positions to help with customer service issues. He says these female leaders have made "a huge difference." For example, "we had serious issues with operations at O'Hare, so we put the best, brightest, most communicative person in the job." That person was Cindy Szadokierski, who began as a customer service agent, moved up into management, found "truly a man's world," but gained the confidence of executives, and has been able to express and activate her need to be herself, be different, be a woman manager. She runs meetings and her team differently from how a man might do it—especially the men who ran things when she herself started out in the airline business (her bosses then were mainly men from military backgrounds), but she is one reason UAL has been coming back strongly from bankruptcy.

In the early 1990s, the perspective of IBM, Deloitte & Touche, UAL, and other similar companies was a gamble. Research into brain-based gender differences was not as well honed as it is now, and there was no way then to prove that awareness of these differences was helpful in shaping management's approach to gender diversity. The feminist movement was very strong, and brain-based differences were suspect in that feminist frame. And the sense that having more female leaders would lead to better financial results was just that—a sense, a notion, without quantitative data to back it up.

Now, we have data showing advantages to the advancement and retention of female leaders when a company uses science-based thinking and tools. We also have the data showing that companies with a good mix of women at the most senior levels generally outperform those without that mix. Over the next decade, we believe most, if not all, companies will begin to look very closely at brain-based gender differences and the specific needs they create in women and men.

Confronting Obstacles to Meeting Women's Needs

Over the last fifteen years, many companies, like those detailed here, have had to break through obstacles to create change. You may be facing many of these obstacles and not know it.

Let's look at the obstacles that impede the process of transformation to a culture more supportive of female leaders. In our research and work we have identified twenty-five obstacles; here we analyze only the most common ones. We also provide immediate, practical strategies for removing the obstacles, should you find them operative in your team or corporation.

Obstacle 1: "We're Doing Fine"

Leaders who present this obstacle say, "Our company is doing fine without more female leaders, so why change?"

A president and CEO of a software company recently told us, "Our executive team has more male than female leaders, and we know this ratio means we are not going to be able to reach out to female consumers as well as we could. At the same time, we're realistic—we know it has taken us a long time to look at these issues because we're doing pretty well financially. For us, there's a gap between knowing we need to make an improvement and acting on it."

The wealth and success of a company is indeed an obstacle. It puts off the retention and advancement of women in executive teams "for a later time." A human resources officer at a software company told Michael, when she hired him for a pilot program to address microinequities, that "We have buy-in for gender diversity and have made a lot of great strides, but this is a very profitable company, so we probably have not done all we can to deal with this issue." The link between bottom line and gender diversity is not understood universally, especially in already profitable companies. It is often difficult to activate a transformation, even when executives know that companies with a balanced mix of male and female leaders increase their bottom line. Without the companies performing a detailed diagnostic of the link between gender balance and profitability, it is hard to push through this obstacle.

Practical Step: Assign a research team in your corporation to gather the data necessary to show the positive effect female leaders have on *your* corporate bottom line. If you are a large company with many similar units, offices, or branches, you may be able to do original research, correlating unit performance with the gender mix of the leadership team. As your research team gathers data, report it as a monthly item in your executive team meetings. All leaders benefit from data analysis, but there are specifically going to be some high-level leaders and executives in the company who perhaps already care morally about women's issues, but still need data to convince them to act.

Once leaders have data showing that improved gender intelligence and balance of men and female leaders improves performance, it is easier for them to initiate programs for improving the ratio of female leaders. Data helps bump an item from "something we'd like to do" to "something we will do."

Obstacle 2: "That Soft Stuff Is Not for Us"

This obstacle is present when leaders say "Gender training is so 'soft,' we are suspicious of it," or "Our company doesn't have time to do touchy-feely gender stuff."

The software company HR director we quoted earlier pointed out this obstacle to learning the secret of women's way of working: the "soft training" obstacle. As she put it, "Gender sensitivity training is often pretty soft; it's kind of touchy-feely. It doesn't work well for a lot of the tech guys in our kind of business. In fact, there's a kind of pessimism sometimes among our HR executive team when we look at how hard it is to get buy-in from a lot of the males and even some of the women to normal gender-sensitivity training."

The feelings of the men and women she referred to are very reasonable feelings. You yourself may have gone to a gender training and thought, "How is this 'soft, touchy-feely' stuff going to help me?" Particularly in technology, engineering, and other "hard facts" fields, there is suspicion about the lack of science in so much of typical gender-sensitivity training (even though that training has been useful in many cases). But now the potential to increase corporate success through knowledge about gender differences need no longer be lost to a nonscientific approach. Both women and men have come to enjoy looking into each other's heads through brain scans in helpful, nonstereotyping, and "hard science" ways. As companies move away from the soft stuff and toward science-based gender training options, we hear comments such as "We have better buy-in from tech-oriented men and women when gender training is based in actual science."

Practical Step: Look carefully for gender training that relies on and understands similarities and differences between the male and the female brain. Make sure the training corporation offers practical tools based in actual science. A reliance on actual science can win over a lot of skeptical men and women to the cause of balanced leadership.

Obstacle 3: "Women Don't Care, So Why Should We?"

These leaders protest, "But women don't want the top jobs, so why force it?" or "At our company, women leave for their own reasons—it's not about our company's policies."

A very strong book on this subject is Sylvia Ann Hewlett's *Off-Ramps, On-Ramps,* based on her studies at Columbia and with the Center for Work-Life Policy, in which she looked carefully at data about women and top jobs. Her studies corroborate our own findings and the findings of nearly every organization studying gender balance in the workplace: a key problem faced by the majority of female leaders at the top levels is not that they don't want senior positions, but that senior positions won't adjust to fit women's needs.

Talented women need corporations to see that many women will indeed travel, relocate, and even, when necessary, work the 24/7 hours sometimes required in senior roles, but only if they as women and leaders have been involved in negotiating when and how they will travel or relocate. Top women need flexibility, and they need to be involved in creating the flexibility in top positions. When top women leave one corporation and go to another, they gain, at the other corporation, the flexibility and valuation they sought as they tried to move up corporate ladders.

Practical Step: Teach leaders that the notion that women don't want top jobs is a myth, not a fact, then build flexibility into how people manage their work schedules so that managers have more control over their own lives. Use as much home office networking as possible, so that top women (and men) can do more of their work online and from home. Work out travel and flex schedules that fit people's lives—women will often give seventy-hour weeks if needed, but are less likely than men to give seventy-hour weeks just because "that's how it's always been done."

Obstacle 4: "So, I'm Supposed to Think Women Are Superior?"

The fear that "gender training is about how women's relating style is superior" presents an obstacle to some men's buy-in.

One executive told us: "Companies will understand that female leadership is needed, so they'll send men to gender sensitivity training. At the training, men will feel bashed or misunderstood—as they are put in a one-down position, made to feel inferior while female leadership styles are being held up as superior—both relationally and in terms of communication. This backfires against women, in the end. It creates problems as we try to address women's issues in the workplace."

This is indeed an obstacle to female leadership expansion. Quite often males do feel that the underlying reason for corporate gender sensitivity or diversity efforts is to get men to change who they are to fit a female relationship mode. Many men disconnect from this because in their workplace the male style is quite effective indeed: very competitive, very profitable, not inferior. When they come to a gender training or a gender issues discussion that implies that the collaborative female relating style is better for business and the male style worse, this defies logic for them. They end up putting conscious and unconscious obstacles in the way of building women-friendliness into leadership programs.

Practical Step: Use training, coaching, and discussions on gender issues that don't polarize men or women, denoting either one as superior. Begin training and discussion about gender issues from a male/female brain difference standpoint—move the "gender culture" of your corporation toward the actual science, so that everyone is speaking from the same language. Seeing the PET and SPECT scans, understanding the biochemistry, talking openly and honestly about natural differences (and exceptions)—these become important determinants in helping leaders, both female and male, to move beyond a "superiority" framework. Once the superiority framework dissolves, women's and men's styles are better understood and thus respected, and male backlash against women's needs dissipates.

Obstacle 5: "That Stuff's Just for Women"

Here you are up against beliefs that "This gender stuff isn't for men, so why should we care?" or "Gender focus is for women only."

Because gender wisdom is often presented in soft and superficial ways, it allows for an avoidance of deeper issues. Men are alienated from gender-intelligent thinking, feeling it is "good for women, maybe, but a waste of men's time." This makes it even harder to deal with gender issues in the workplace. Men don't buy into needing to help the workplace shift to incorporate women's styles.

When HR teams or other mentors present gender training or gender diversity programs as being mainly or only about advancing women, men (and even some women who are already at the top) can be turned off. They may even lash back against the gender programs. Dealing with women's issues requires corporations to also deal with men's issues, as the issues of women and men are intertwined. (In Chapter Nine, we'll go into the work-related gender issues that men face.)

Practical Step: To "sell" gender balance to your teammates, leaders, and managers, show them that it is not for women only. What are men's needs? What are men's issues? Ask these questions as vehemently as you ask questions about women's needs and issues. Also, set up a gender task force that is composed of both women and men and co-led by a female and male leader.

Obstacle 6: Good Old Boy Networks

Women complain of this obstacle: "There are male-only activities women are not invited to, and thus we as women are isolated from leadership."

You'll note that we have listed the "good old boy" obstacle sixth, not first or second. Forty years ago we could certainly have listed it first, but the workplace has changed. Although some men *do* network with men to the exclusion of women (as women do with men), this obstacle is not the impediment to transformation and success that it once was. As Maria Ferris of IBM told us in 2007, "Even in 1997, the top barrier to women's advancement at IBM was the male-dominated culture. Today, it is not. This is not bad for a company that has 360,000 employees."

Sharon Roberts, a gender and leadership trainer out of Dallas, made the choice to reorient her gender leadership trainings to a science-based framework. After providing a training in the heating and cooling industry, she told us, "I'm not finding as much of the good old boy network in the workplace as I once did, but even when I do, using the brain science has helped. The eyes of both male and female CEOs light up. They see the bottom-line applications immediately."

A mother and grandmother, and married to her husband Lon for almost four decades, Sharon said, "One thing I've learned is that most of the male CEOs I work with are fathers, many have daughters, many are married—they aren't thinking male dominance or man-against-woman. They want the best for their daughters and wives and sisters, and they want to make a good world for their sons."

Male-exclusive clubs and activities have diminished since the changes brought by the feminist movement, and their power to harm women's advancement continues to diminish through the new gender evolution. But if you see a good old boy network around you in *your* corporation, you can bet it is an obstacle to your overall and long-term corporate growth.

Practical Step: Three practical steps can be taken simultaneously:

1. Establish a women's mentoring system (see Chapter Ten).
2. Use science in trainings. Science speaks to many men, even "good old boys," at core levels that other, softer trainings often do not. Helping them to understand the content from Chapters One through Three and use the GenderTools of Chapters Four through Seven can create "Aha!" moments for them.
3. Form a gender task force or modify your existing one to provide diagnostics and surveys that look at subtle gender biases, not just overt ones. The results of this focus can be brought to all your leaders, through reports and in-house studies. We provide a partial list of gender biases in the next Try This box.

Obstacle 7: "We Don't Have a Problem"

This obstacle surfaces in statements like "We don't have gender issues" or "We've been there, done that—gender issues are resolved in our corporation."

You may be working in a corporation in which, indeed, women are retained and advancing quite well. This and the other obstacles may not seem to fit with your daily work life. You may experience a sense or a feeling in your company: "Been there, done that." Last year, perhaps, or two years ago, a book study was completed, or a task force formed; some recommendations were made, some good things happened. There are other issues to look at now—the gender work has been done.

Maybe it has, but maybe it hasn't. And even if it has, gender issues are not single issues that go away. With each new set of male and female leaders and employees, the gender intelligence shifts, the gender issues move a little bit in a new direction. Companies we've worked with stay on top of gender balance issues year after year. Gender has been with us for a million years or so. It is a constant part of work life.

Try This
Track Ongoing Issues of Gender Bias

One measure of where things stand for your corporation could appear in this survey of overt and covert gender biases. Use this short tool to check in on where things are in your corporation. Let it help you determine if there are significant issues right now in your team. One quick approach is to e-mail it to all your leaders and see how they respond.

1. Does overt sexism exist in our leadership teams? Are women stereotyped? Is there a woman on the team right now who feels put down, constantly devalued, left out?
2. Are women given special treatment, as if they will fail and must be protected? Is there a particular woman treated this way?
3. Is there denial of women's concerns in our leadership team? For example, are women struggling and leaving the corporation but no one will admit it?
4. Does the corporation have enough female role models in high positions?

5. Do men in high positions mentor women (mentoring is *not* the same as treating with kid gloves)?

6. In meetings, are women assigned traditional roles such as taking notes, or called on to speak less than men are? Are men given credit for women's ideas? Are women expected to organize social functions?

7. Are women judged (by both female and male leaders) by a double standard? For example, do they have to work twice as hard as a man to get the same advancement and promotion?

8. Are women discriminated against because they have or may have children? For example, is a qualified woman not promoted because she may have a child in the future?

9. Are women judged as a group? For example, when one woman fails, is it attributed to her whole gender?

If you send these questions (or others like them) to your management team, you may find confidential answers coming to you from colleagues who feel subtle or overt biases as micro or macro inequities in the whole corporate culture. You may also find that many survey participants seem to be saying there is gender bias not in the whole corporation, but specifically involving one or more people. This can help you localize and treat the issue.

And remember, not only can man be in denial, but there can be denial among women at the top. As you look at your company's ability to retain and advance women, don't be surprised if some women at the very top of the corporation say, "There aren't women's issues anymore," or "We don't want to deal with issues as 'women's' issues—we don't want it to look like women need special treatment."

Women who have made it to CEO positions may have had to fight to get there during a time when the workplace dealt with gender from either a traditionalist or feminist frame. These women fought hard, as individuals, with little help! They often do not notice now—from their top position—that thousands of women below them are struggling, and many are being lost to the corporation. Any of us who rise to the top can sometimes forget how we got there.

This forgetfulness is just one of the factors that can lead women in your corporation to report as much gender bias among other women as among men—or even more! Sometimes men can be more supportive of women than women are, especially if the men have come to value the strength and power of a particular woman through her proving herself to them.

Try This
Become Aware of Your Team's Stage of Awareness

These "stages of awareness" present another practical tool you can use immediately to help you explore obstacles to women's retention and advancement in leadership in your workplace. This is a framework we use at the outset of our work with companies.

We have identified four stages of corporate gender awareness: denial, acknowledgment, frustration, and partnership or congruence. All of us as individuals, as well as every team and corporation, can identify with being at each stage at different times. A group or company can actually be in more than one stage at the same time, depending on the specific issues it is trying to analyze. For instance, the company can be in denial about one area of gender balance, but be in congruence about another. What is your leadership team's stage of awareness?

To use this as a tool on your leadership team, talk together about which stage(s) your team or company is in. This conversation is best conducted after you've looked at the previous seven obstacles. The obstacles give your team a common language for looking at stages.

- *Stage 1: Denial.* Which, if any, of the obstacles or gender biases described earlier would you say your team is denying? List the areas of denial specifically.

    You may see denial around you from traditionalist managers who say, "We are doing a good job of treating men and women equally. I'm not interested in hearing research on why this isn't good enough anymore."

    You may hear denial from people operating in the feminist frame. That frame is in denial with respect to gender differences. These individuals might say, "The research about brain-based differences is just stereotyping," or "Men's issues matter less than women's," or "There's no brain difference between women and men."

- *Stage 2: Acknowledgment.* In this stage, individuals and companies push through denial and see that gender intelligence is crucial and gender balance improves the bottom line. A combination of internal data gathering and external assistance generally makes this stage possible. A hidden gift also makes it possible: team awareness of the need to be fully honest. Men come to acknowledge their strengths and weaknesses, as do women. Women and men begin to have conversations that go deeper.

    In the acknowledgment stage we realize that by denying differences we misinterpret men and women. Women begin to be honest about the fact that they have been seeing men through the lens of their own way of thinking, which led to misinterpretations. One common "Aha!" moment during this stage for women regards men and winning. A woman manager, during the acknowledgment stage, might say, "Men do seem to want to win a lot. I understand now that it's part of how men get a sense of accomplishment. I like winning, but I get a sense of accomplishment by building relationships and influencing others." This acknowledgment language moves beyond any judging or blaming.

Men too become honest in their acknowledgments, but often in their own way. They will say things like, "Well, now that you mention it, the way Judy leads does have its advantages." Or "The way I do things isn't the only way—I have some things to learn from Claire." Or, jokingly, "I'm not in denial! I just wish it was all about winning, but okay, yeah, I get that I don't understand women consumers like Cindy does." When men acknowledge hard-wired gender differences, they often begin to try to honestly envision how to best use women's talents.

- *Stage 3: Frustration.* Often a leadership team will gain an empowering feeling of resolve—gender diagnostics will have been completed, issues raised and honestly laid out, male and female brain better understood—but then the realization comes that a lot is not being dealt with, impediments still exist, obstacles aren't being removed; the promise of the early goal setting and the anticipation of "finally solving our problems" diminishes into the reality of how broad and often difficult is the task of gender-intelligent thinking and gender-balanced leadership.

  Sometimes, during this stage, leaders who gained insight during the acknowledgment stage will revert to old stereotyping, as a defense against the diminished enjoyment they now feel. One woman we worked with in this stage had spent years telling women they needed to be tougher, play by the rules, behave like men to get ahead. She had even disliked women, saying women were "high maintenance in leadership, and couldn't cut it in sales either." As her corporation gained gender intelligence and worked toward balance in stage 2, she let go of this thinking, seeing the flaw in it; but later, when she entered a time of frustration with the slowness of her corporation's development of gender balance, she regained her previous frustrations and added more; she became frustrated with both women *and men.*

The frustration stage needs a great deal of patience. Because hard-wired gender differences have been building in us for about one million years, and because our workplaces are stress-filled environments wherein solutions to human relationship issues cannot be quick, the development of gender intelligence and gender balance generally takes a large corporation a number of years. We must expect some frustration along the way, and mentors and coaches become very important in this stage.

- *Stage 4: Partnership or Congruence.* As you've seen in this chapter, a number of individuals and corporations push through the first three stages and reach the fourth. In this stage, a corporate culture develops within companies that lets people be themselves—whether they want to do high fives after a deal or prefer to demur. Differences and diversity may still be frustrating at times, but now they become even more powerfully advantageous to a company.

Companies and teams that gain congruence tend to see clear markers of male-female partnership and women's partnership in corporate culture. Among these markers are

- Increased work/life balance
- Open discussion about retention of women as a core issue
- Ongoing gender intelligence training
- Advancement and use of mentoring and coaching systems
- Realistic options for women and men with children

One of the most telling markers of a leadership team in the congruence stage shows up in its ability to integrate women's relational and family needs into corporate success. The majority of women and men will, during their work life, marry and have children. What will the company do about this? (In Chapter Nine, we'll look at this issue for men.) We asked Mary Beth Backof at PricewaterhouseCoopers, a firm that has won numerous diversity awards, how they handled these issues. She told us,

As we moved through stages of awareness on gender balance, one thing we focused on in particular was to retain women through their child-bearing years. We were the first firm to have part-time partners—a phrase that seemed like an oxymoron in the eighties, but we have shown it can work. When I had my two kids it was up to me to run around trying to find a nanny, but now that Employee Assistance Programs (EAPs) have come along they can provide a lot of help. One challenge was the lack of female role models so we had conferences to showcase the success of women.

One thing you don't often hear about in the professional context is the difficulty professional women have meeting people. I met my future husband at the firm but because of rules against nepotism we had to date secretly for six years. When we decided to get married they changed the rules so that we could both continue to work at the firm, but warned us that we both couldn't make partner. Then as we both reached the level to make partner they changed the rules again so that neither of us would have to quit. So the firm has evolved to remove barriers that stood in the way of women.

There are many challenges I faced in my career and to some extent women still face. A man once asked me, "Your husband's a partner, why do you work?" Sometimes there is an unspoken feeling from men that you are taking opportunities away from them that they need more badly than you.

Getting women to the senior ranks has been hampered because women, often women with children, will sit too long in a given position while men move more strategically through leadership roles. The succession planning committee looks at the candidates and finds the ones with the best experience are all men. So we've been consciously picking young women and moving them to higher-level positions more rapidly.

The Quiet Evolution

The leaders and companies featured in this chapter have moved through the stages of awareness toward congruence and success. These leaders and their companies have decided to be satisfied only when gender balance has been achieved. They use brain-based information and tools to open the minds of both women and men to the full potential of each gender at all corporate levels.

We have hinted throughout this book that we feel there is a gender evolution occurring in corporations. We've presented a historical framework for it, noting that our workplaces began as preindustrial or industrial structures in which it was commonly believed that women and men were inherently different, but this belief led to women being underused. The sphere of work then moved into a feminist framework in which women and men were believed to not be inherently different—this framework led to many gains for women, but has also become stagnant and even suspect to many people. Now a more evolved brain-based gender intelligence movement among corporations, communities, and policy makers is swiftly gaining understanding of the broad spectrum of the male and female brain, and innovating tools from across that spectrum to retain and advance women.

This new evolutionary phase of gender development does not pit present against past, but instead carries forward the best of human history. This gender evolution unites retention of women in the workplace with new science and leading-edge gender thinking.

The leaders and corporations that progress through the stages of denial, acknowledgment, and frustration to congruence and partnership do not create perfect gender environments; they do not suddenly erase all stereotypes, all problems, all issues—but they do accomplish amazing goals, and they move not only their corporations but the industrial world as a whole toward a fresh approach, a future for women that accesses their full potential as human beings, allowing them to live and work in partnership with men.

A recent Gallup survey asked 1.7 million men and women in 101 companies in 63 countries whether they felt they "had the opportunity to do their best every day at their job." Only 20 percent of employees said yes. Over the next decades, as awareness of gender intelligence increases and corporations move toward partnership and congruence at the highest levels, that percentage will increase. In the companies featured in this chapter, enjoyment of work and productivity are higher than the Gallup average. When companies care about what women need and how they succeed, the landscape of data and everyday work life becomes very different indeed. (See the Notes and Resources for more on the Gallup survey and studies and articles of related interest.)

Gender issues are very human issues, and we are poised in this new millennium to take them on. And gender issues are not just women's issues—they are also men's issues. In the next chapter we will look at men's strengths, men's issues, and how to maximize male potential even better than we are doing now.

Situational Exercise

For Men

Imagine how it feels to be a woman in this workplace. Write down three challenges that you would face.

For Women

Write down three challenges you face in this workplace, and note how you feel about them. Be specific.

If it is possible and appropriate in your learning team, compare notes. It is useful for men to go first, then for women to follow. This helps show seen and unseen biases that men may not have realized they carried.

Fourth Principle and Task of Balanced Leadership

Principle 4: Gender balance is crucial to retaining and advancing women of talent in a corporation. When we apply science-based insight about gender, we alter corporations to fully advance women—through understanding, and through intervention when necessary.

Task/Actions 4: Apply gender biology to your workplace by looking at the obstacles women face in your corporation, misunderstandings men fall into when dealing with talented women, and lack of work/life balance. See women as powerful, and listen with openness to what women are saying about what they need.

Summary

1. Women's talents are crucial to workplace success—they lead to greater financial success in a corporation.
2. Many corporations have already shown the ROI of applying brain-based gender science in the workplace.
3. Women's needs are often unrecognized or not adequately addressed in the workplace.
4. Women send signals of doubt that we can read and deal with effectively.
5. Corporations face a number of removable obstacles regarding retention and advancement of female talent.
6. Four stages of awareness of brain-based gender differences show up in companies working on gender issues.
7. Unintentional bias against women exists and can be recognized and resolved by leadership teams.
8. Businesses are poised for change. As corporations change, gains for women, men, and the corporations themselves become quite specific and measurable.

Helping Men
Recognizing Men's Leadership Strengths and Solving Issues Men Face

We as women leaders have as much to learn about men as they do about us.

—JUDY MEPHAM, XEROX

THE SETTING WAS A MULTIDAY WORKSHOP OF WOMEN AND MEN at a major corporation. The task to fulfill that morning: meet in small groups and make lists of (1) the strengths men bring to leadership and the workplace and (2) the issues men face in leadership and the workplace today. In this workshop we had already looked closely at brain differences and also at women's strengths and issues.

As we were getting under way, a man joked, "Men's strengths? That won't fill up much of a page!" Some of the leaders winced at this humor, but it revealed, as humor often can, hidden feelings and experiences. As we would learn later when we looked at men's issues and needs, this leadership team, like many others, didn't realize how many men had complex feelings they could articulate, at first, only with jokes.

Much of the gender discussion involves women's needs and issues. Men's strengths are often forgotten in these discussions, and men's needs and issues in the workplace put aside. This is ironic, of course, because for centuries men were the center of discussion.

Over the last two and a half decades, both Michael and Barbara have developed and implemented programs that help men. Our diagnostic surveys have included equal time for men to articulate what is happening for them. We have found that the evolution of gender intelligence requires as much powerful clarity about who men are as who women are. Men are involved, especially in this postindustrial age, in massive transformations of role focus and personal development. A corporation that is looking at women's issues succeeds best by also understanding men, especially the strengths the male brain brings inherently to leadership and the issues that emerge for men as they apply their strengths. IBM, for instance, garnered its success in gender intelligence evolution by bringing men into all dialogues. As Maria Ferris told Barbara, IBM launched a men's task force along with its women's task forces, including a White Male Task Force. IBM knows that all constituent groups are important to globalization and success as a corporation.

Try This
Understand Men's Strengths

Take a moment to pay attention to what you already know or feel about men's strengths.

For Women

- Imagine you are the man in your workplace that you admire the most. What are your strengths? The secrets of your success? Write down the top three that come to mind.

For Men

- Write down your top three strengths—your secrets of success. If possible, share in your next team meeting the results of this exercise.

In this chapter, we will look carefully first at men's strengths and how to maximize them, then at men's issues that may exist right now in your corporation and leadership team—issues that can negatively affect leadership, long-term partnership, and overall corporate success, from a male point of view.

Clarifying and Maximizing Men's Strengths

When we ask both male and female leaders to list men's strengths, here are some of the many that appear:

1. Staying focused on the task, keeping teams focused
2. Humor, lots of it
3. Seeing designs, ideas in big visions, legacies
4. Constantly testing and being competitive (this can be both good and bad)
5. Thinking in terms of systems organization—men protect the system to the very end
6. Risk taking
7. Working well in teams, if the teams don't waste time; not gossiping too much
8. Accepting you once you've proven yourself, but you have to prove yourself
9. Capacity to be a good mentor, if you specifically ask for what you need
10. Love of gadgets, loving to move around, creating excitement
11. Being compassionate and caring, in their own male way
12. Not hanging on to things or holding grudges

Perhaps you have noticed many of these strengths in many of the men around you. Each of these strengths and assets can be understood in parallel with female strengths, and each can be seen as necessary for workplace success. Rather than look at all twelve, let's look carefully at one primal strength that is a key to male authentic leadership and foundational to gender balance. Gaining gender intelligence on this male/female difference in leadership focus can be something of a revelation regarding shared leadership. For many men, this strength is unconscious and not something they can describe well in words; for many women, this strength can be confusing. For all of us, it is crucial to discover or rediscover this primal asset men bring to leadership and life. This strength is a lighthouse—it will never go away, and we don't want it to. It is one of the primary reasons our corporations succeed.

Competitive Systems Thinking and Systems Protection

Charles Darwin wrote the following assessment about men he observed in 1871: "A tribe including many members who, from possessing in high degree the spirit of patriotism, fidelity, obedience, courage and sympathy, were always ready to aid one another, and to sacrifice themselves for the common good; would be victorious over most other tribes, and this would be natural selection."

Darwin has become, in our modern day, a polarizing and politicized figure. A few strands of his theories have been the center of many debates, and the bulk of his work forgotten. This is unfortunate, actually, because his studies were rigorous, and his understanding of male/female difference, without the help of PET scans or biochemical analyses, was very advanced.

Fortunately for our work in gender and leadership, his observation of differences in leadership patterns between males and females has been analyzed by neuroscientists and proven correct. We now understand that *male leaders (in general) tend to focus their loyalty and obedience on protecting the larger competitive system they engage in, and base their compassion and empathy for others on others' performance within that larger system. Their empathy is not as individualized as women's empathy, and their strength in natural selection lies directly in this difference.*

What do we mean by this? Male biochemistry and brain structure, as well as socialization, create a leadership style in men that shows primal devotion to the overall protection of a competitive system itself—that is, the "big picture." Male leaders tend to protect the corporation's success not through caring immediately for an individual's feelings and emotions but through the breaking down and building up of competitive relationships that support a large system of accomplishment.

Female leaders (in general) tend to empathize with individuals more quickly than males do, protecting the overall system of the workplace through empathic response with individuals who are crucial to the success of the system. Females care a lot about the big picture, but female leaders will also put more effort into balancing that concern with taking care of individuals in the system than male leaders tend to do.

In his research on male/female behavior, Michael has identified this difference as a contrast between two brain- and biochemistry-based attributes: women's *direct empathy* and men's *aggression nurturance*. Women tend to nurture through direct empathy with individuals in immediate situations. Men tend to nurture in deference to the aggression/competition hierarchy to which they have become loyal.

The English psychologist Simon Baron-Cohen (*The Essential Difference*) has proven the universality of this male/female leadership difference, pointed out years ago by Darwin, by using brain scans. American psychologist Shelley Taylor (*The Tending Instinct*) has proven it through oxytocin and brain chemistry research. The empathy/aggression difference is wired into us via brain structures, blood flow in the brain, biochemistry, and, of course, socialization.

An interesting manifestation of this male/female difference revealed itself recently at a division of the Department of Justice in Canada that we were working with. During a difficult case involving family law, two sides of an argument split along gender lines. The women argued about the needs of individual family members if a certain decision were to be taken. The men said the law was very clear and must be upheld for the legal system to have any integrity. We may not like the outcome, they said, but the law is the law. That is crystal clear systems thinking among men.

You have probably seen this primal difference in your own leadership team (and certainly there will be exceptions, too). Jack Welch is a celebrity example of a male leader who puts the system above the individual. In his success model, the worst 20 percent of performers in a company must be let go and then replaced every year; in his view, the bottom 20 percent drag down the system. Who these people are cannot matter as much to the executive, he argues, as their effect on the corporation as a system. Many companies have emulated Jack Welch's leadership style, and done quite well for it.

??? Did You Know ???

Men and Women Care About Individuals Differently

Even in caring about individuals—men do care about individuals!—you may still see leadership differences that are primal to the authentic maleness and femaleness we are getting at here. Understanding these can help allow men to fulfill their potential as leaders.

Male leaders often care by (1) "doing big things" for the hurt person that may, in the end, give the person comfort from afar, or (2) by trying to push the "weaker link" to improve, buck up, get moving, "not wallow"—a leadership strategy that may seem, at first, painful to the person's self-esteem, but can in fact help increase it and simultaneously keep the system in focus.

One poignant example of the first strategy showed up when we were working with the leadership team at a law firm. This team suddenly learned that one of their female partners had cancer and a low likelihood of survival. The women on the team immediately got on the phone, talking to the sick woman and other people in her support network. The men held back, respecting the ill woman's privacy and not wanting to intrude when the person was so vulnerable, but they considered how to help her "from afar." While the female partners took turns visiting her, the male CEO got her an apartment close to the hospital, never speaking to her directly about it. He wanted to protect her viability in the system—she was a trusted and needed leader, and he didn't want to lose her as an asset. Both men and women cared, but how they expressed that caring showed up very differently.

So it is also that when a person on a team is weak in performance, males don't tend to spend as much time helping that person along. Men are more likely to figure, "A few chances, then you're out." Males see the system as aggressive and inherently competitive. There's no use coddling someone who can't keep up.

This authentic male way of leading is one of the pivotal reasons men and women have had such difficulty over the last five decades in working in gender-balanced partnership. This primal leadership difference, when practiced with the other gender, can feel alien and even dangerous. When men try to help women by competing, pushing, prodding, making them feel weak so they'll get strong, women often must become a third sex—or else they just check out of the corporation.

Gender intelligence and gender balance require deep understanding of men, because the way men work in systems, empathize, and care about self-esteem won't go away. To hope that it will, or to not focus on it, diminishes the power of a company, and leads to men checking out of evolutionary gender dialogues.

In the area of self-esteem building, our popular culture and many of our corporations (especially female leaders in corporations) have widely misinterpreted the male systems-protection asset, and in so doing inadvertently missed the power and importance of primal differences in male and female self-esteem building. This has significantly impacted women's abilities to gain from what men have to teach and to get stronger in corporate leadership.

Let's look closely at this for a moment. Have you noticed that for a few decades now, it has been suggested that the male aggression-nurturance approach is worse for a person's self-esteem than the female direct-empathy approach—that is, that the competitive male is *hurting* self-esteem by being hard on individuals, or not sympathizing enough, whereas the empathic female is *building* self-esteem by sympathizing more? "He's not being very sensitive to his coworker's self-esteem," you may have heard someone say. "He's so critical—he doesn't have any empathy."

Although certainly any man or woman can be far too critical, what we're getting at here is our popular and corporate tendency to see self-esteem building as something that only happens when people are sensitive to a person's immediate feelings. In this way of seeing self-esteem, if a person fails or is hurting, he or she is best nurtured back to strength by someone who listens to the person's feelings and thus allows the person to express the hurt and move forward.

Male leaders often see self-esteem building as quite different from this feeling-based self-improvement. They have seen it differently since they were little boys. They tend to think of *self-confidence building* more than *self-esteem raising*.

A male CEO in his thirties talked in one of our seminars about the movie *Batman Begins*, which he had just seen with his kids. He brought up some lines from the movie to illustrate what we might mean by male self-confidence building.

The Father: Son, why do we fall?
The Son: Why?
The Father: To learn to pick ourselves back up again.

As the group of leaders discussed these lines, both the women and men understood that the father's job in this context is to inspire and push the son to "pick himself up"—to become strong enough as quickly as possible to help himself up, with little thought at all to his own hurt feelings in the moment. In *Batman Begins* (worth renting to see a fascinating illustration of male development), the way in which the son handles those feelings is to direct them into a projection of his demons, his nemesis, his enemy. The best leader, he understands, must build up his own and others' self-confidence by learning to be independent of emotional excess, concentrating and focused on challenges, and able to strongly function within a system that needs him for its survival against major odds.

For men, this is often what a corporation is, and the male brain and biochemistry are servants of this corporate system. From the point of view of the male leader, his form of nurturing actually raises self-confidence—by forcing a "weaker" underperformer to perform, to reach the goal, to be a part of the strong group and not part of a weak group (or to get weeded out); he sees himself as helping the weak performer "get moving, get with the system," and thus not only perform but also gain the self-confidence that comes from protecting the system. From an evolutionary perspective, this natural approach to self-esteem building and systems protection spurs leaders like Jack Welch to cut the bottom 20 percent as an innovation that entails complete systems protection and self-esteem building, from a male viewpoint.

In our work with corporate leaders, we find this primal difference in self-confidence building and systems protection lies at the root of many issues that women have with men. Just as many men do not deeply understand the power and strength of women's leadership assets, many women are frustrated with men's almost myopic systems protection and apparent lack of sympathy. Unless a particular woman was brought up with a number of brothers, or otherwise had access to large and passionate groups of males at work or play on a constant basis, the male way of challenging each other to build each other up can become a pivot point of judgment against males.

At the same time, the direct empathy versus aggression-nurturance difference is one of the primal reasons it can be so difficult for male leaders to immediately allow female leaders like Pam Gomez Gil into the fold. Male leaders expect long-term proof from the women (and any up-and-coming men as well) that they are *protectors of the system,* not just selfishly pursuing their own personal needs or a small group's emotional self-esteem. A woman working with these male leaders can easily feel she must become a man who puts the system above the person in order to succeed. And quite often it can seem to her that men selfishly don't care about individuals except those on their own male team. Often female leaders will say, "Men are selfish and egotistical—they will trample on anyone to gain personal power."

Although for some narcissistic men (and women) this assessment may be quite true, for many males their own personal feeling is not selfishness but a *selfless* imperative to protect the system that "provides nourishment for all." This is what Darwin was trying to get at when he described the tribe of men. Men will often not understand why women call them selfish. Often, in fact, men will think female leaders are selfish about "this woman or that man"; that is, male leaders will think the woman is not protecting "the system that feeds us all," but instead spending too much time caring about herself and her colleagues' feelings. Men will, thus, see her as betraying the larger system's strength.

In all that we're saying here, there can be exceptions, and there can be both male and female leaders who abuse their power. These are givens, and our evolutionary analysis of the primal male/female difference is not useful if it becomes an excuse for bad behavior.

What we hope you will take away from this analysis is its usefulness in deepening your gender intelligence as you work to solve leadership issues between genders in your corporation. The GenderTools in this book become even more useful when you keep in mind the primal difference between female and male leaders. The GenderTools help bridge gaps and build on strengths. Gender-intelligent companies will often use this information about primal leadership style differences to look closely at new hires for executive and management teams. They will sometimes need to make sure that for every Pam Gomez Gil on the team there is a Jack Welch, and vice versa.

One Team's Story: A System Protected

A Los Angeles–based global company in the retail business had been very successful, resulting in the stock shooting up 400 percent in just five years. It was a success that stoked the ambitions of some of the leadership team, especially the COO, who decided to try to uproot the CEO and take over. With a cadre of five other partners, he decided to mount a coup. He and his chosen group began doing deals without the CEO's knowledge and made promises to third parties that they said would be delivered on as soon as the CEO was gone.

The CEO heard some rumors, but couldn't believe, at first, that anything seriously bad was going on. Ultimately, however, someone called the whistle-blower line in the corporation with names and dates detailing the COO's lavish spending on bonuses to his group for bogus expense claims. The CEO initiated an investigation, and the legal team responsible for the investigation discovered an extensive chain of e-mail messages revealing the conspiracy. One night, security found the COO deleting e-mails and shredding documents.

This company decided to get gender help when its leadership team (ten men and one woman) was in disrepair. Some of the members of the team had acted unethically, some illegally, and some with far too much attention to their own ambitions. The COO himself, as he was being fired, claimed the stock would tank because the company could not live without him. Other members of the team quit, were fired, or were prosecuted. The COO and his cadre illustrated a dark side to hypercompetitiveness and ambition, and the whole corporation suffered from the machinations of these few people.

At the same time, male systems protection kicked in immediately. Once the worst culprits had been identified by the CEO, he reached into management to find the people he could trust. Five of the male SVPs took a stand and came to his side. "We're here to turn this ship around," they promised. "Quitting is not an option." "We'll get this done no matter what." "We will not lose our company because of a few bad apples." "It's time to clean out the system and regain values."

They did indeed purge the system. They met nearly every day to plan out how to restore the system to proper conduct. There were brief discussions to determine which of the COO's buddies were peripheral to the conspiracy and which were central—brief discussions of whether perhaps the peripheral culprits ought to get a second chance—but then it was unanimously decided that the leadership team and system were more important than these people's individual careers. They had to be fired along with the other culprits.

Once this purge had taken place, the CEO and this team launched mandatory workshops and seminars in which team members started speaking the truth to each other about what was going on and strategized on how to accelerate breakthrough results. There were symbolic acts to emphasize the extent of the change.

The culture did change dramatically: these five SVPs were deemed "our enlightened heroes," the dangerous individuals were swept away, the system was protected and quickly restored. It's a different kind of company now, a company of high trust, collaboration, and integrity—and, walking around on the top floor, you can feel the difference.

And the COO was wrong—without him, the stock rose another 82 percent.

The Risk-Taking Assets That Men Bring to Large-Systems Leadership

The story of the Los Angeles–based company shows a male team responding immediately to a crisis in the system and moving quickly to fix the problems, without care for the feelings of the individuals who needed to be purged. It also hints at an area of male energy and biology—male risk taking—that can get a system into trouble *and* be a great asset in leadership. Let's look at it closely.

To explore aggression nurturance and male groupings without exploring male risk taking would be to look at only one side of the coin. Males are by nature more likely to aggressively and quickly take physical and hierarchical risks than are females. The COO is an example of this risk taking. It can be very interesting to talk about this risk taking in leadership teams, because at first it may seem contradictory to say, "Males are loyal to and try to protect the system" while also saying, "Males are more likely than females to take significant individual risks, many of which may threaten to break apart the system!"

In the end, we must state that males are both more likely to protect the large-group system at the expense of individual feelings and yet, at the same time, more likely to aggressively take risks that challenge the structure of the system.

A female leader told us why she thinks this goes on: "To me, men are driven by two different instincts, and that's what makes them exciting. On the one hand, they will do anything to protect the people they care about and the system they've bought into. On the other hand, they are never satisfied with who they are or what the system is—at least, maybe, not until their first heart attack. Until then, men just keep pushing, challenging, taking risks, and thinking they are invulnerable."

As this leader talked in the workshop, men were not offended. They got what she was saying. She had captured something universal.

You have probably intuited in your everyday life that some males, like the COO in the established system, take many risks—risks that many women may not be as prone to take. In biological terms, this can lead to shorter life spans for men, unethical conduct, unfortunate crises in systems, and a number of other issues—yet it is also a vast asset integral to any corporation.

In trying to help define the way in which male risk taking is an asset, Pam Gomez Gil gave us this observation from her thirty years of leading technology corporations:

Some women, of course, are very willing to take risks, but compared to men, I've found that women often wait to take a "reasonable risk"' rather than an outright risk. I mean that women leaders are more likely to take the risk when they secretly know it isn't a risk—when they've done the backup work to prove their idea. Men, on the other hand, are more likely to just "go for it."

The male way of doing it is quite an asset, because for women, there is a Bermuda Triangle: women don't take as many risks, therefore don't make as many mistakes in a possibly friendly environment, therefore don't learn from the mistakes, therefore don't gain certain long-term advantages. Men take more risks, make more mistakes, learn certain things more quickly, and in some cases, gain significant advantages for themselves, their executive teams, and their corporations.

Pam has seen something you may see around you: men taking the risks they need to take in order to climb up corporate ladders. Yes, they make mistakes, but that's part of the asset building: they and people around them learn from the mistakes. Men generally take "smart risks" when they see a way those risks can, with some likelihood, increase their status in the team itself or their team's status in the larger system. Men will also, if significant status is to be gained *and* if they see the existing system as deeply flawed, take risks that may break down facets of the system so it can be rebuilt toward greater (even riskier) success positions.

The prevailing evolutionary theory for why men seem more prone to risk taking (from jumping out of airplanes to stepping in front of bullets to making risky social and corporate maneuvers) borrows from both male/female brain difference and biochemical difference. As contemporary neuroscience has shown, testosterone is a high-risk hormone—even women with higher amounts of testosterone take more physical and social risks! Testosterone, along with the chemical vasopressin (and lower levels of oxytocin), appear to focus male acumen more constantly on territorial protection, assessment, and hierarchical expansion than females do. Also, as we've explored in previous chapters, the male brain focuses a great deal of mental energy and power on where men fit in hierarchies and systems. In general, men take more of the sort of risks we're discussing than women do, and among competitive male executives there can be even higher testosterone levels and even more ability to expand territory and status through risk taking.

Male and female socialization most certainly play a role in how much an individual woman or man will take hierarchical, social, personal, and even impulsive risks. At the same time, the depth of men's biological drive to take risks is, like male systems protection, a lighthouse, and smart managers and executives gain a great deal from the men they lead when they help those men take risks and protect systems at the same time. On your leadership team, we hope you'll equally discuss the male asset of systems protection through sacrifice of the individual for the group *and* the male asset of systems disruption through individual risk taking that is potentially harmful to group cohesion but advances men up hierarchies. In this paradox lies a great deal of the "light" in human nature, and there is no single strategy that solves or fixes the paradox. It is a part of nature, a piece of the gender whole that each leadership team must discuss and make decisions about so that risk taking—which is one of the foundational elements of a successful business—remains a constant asset for both women and men. How you train and mentor it will determine, to a great extent, the success of the men and women in your corporation.

It can be very helpful for leadership teams to take questions about male risk taking into the GenderTool on mentoring and coaching in Chapter Ten. Male risk taking is one of the key things you will be called on, as a man or woman, to mentor and coach in your workforce.

Understanding Issues Men Face in Leadership

An executive recently told us, "You have to put this anonymously in your book because it's not politically correct in my company, but we have a big problem here—the male bashing has gotten bad. Men feel like they can't say anything or make any jokes for fear of getting trounced by the system we have in place." This executive came up to us during a break after a piece we were doing in the training regarding primal differences in systems, self-esteem building, and risk taking. As we talked, it was clear he had experienced an "Aha!" moment regarding how male bashing can occur from deep misunderstandings regarding men's behavior and men's strengths. He continued, "I think what happens sometimes is that men are trying to be their best in the best way they know, but it scares some of the women and so they bash us. The risks men take, the way men develop self-esteem—it makes such sense—but all of us are confused about each other, and it shows in how we overreact and bash."

It was very important that this executive spoke up, even if privately, about his experiences. Male leaders will often not articulate as well as female leaders the feelings they are having. Both male brain structure and socialization contribute to this reticence. Men will often sit on issues until they fester. When they've festered, the men will often act out in order to be heard—and this acting out can cause them and others a great deal of pain.

As whole systems, corporations will often neglect to deal with men's issues because most people in the corporation (including many of the women!) tacitly believe, "Men are tough, they can take it, they'll work it out," or "They have it all, why are they whining?" Men are indeed tough, often single-minded in their sacrifice of self for the system, and by nature quite often uncommunicative, internalizing their confusion—especially their confusion about women. But men's issues must be addressed openly. To do so is evolutionary. It opens up authentic leadership expansion for both men and women. Specifically, if an executive team has become enlightened concerning women's issues, discussion of men's issues becomes the absolutely necessary next step. If male issues are not addressed, there is a sense in the corporation of "something missing." That missing fairness becomes a drag on helping women: men don't buy into helping women because they feel that the dialogue is one-sided. They feel disenfranchised from gender issues. Advocates of women don't want that—they want men to know that their issues are taken seriously, with mutual respect.

Try This
Identify Challenges Men Face

Take a moment to pay attention to men's issues.

For Women

- Imagine you are the man in your workplace right now. What are your most significant challenges? Write down the top three.

For Men

- What are the challenges you face? Write down the top three.
- If possible and appropriate, share in your next team meeting the results of this exercise. It is often useful for the men to go first, then the women to follow. This allows the men to discuss their issues in their own form of articulation at the outset.

Men's Issues (What Men Need)

There is an interesting difference in our survey work with women and men that tells us a lot about effective ways to handle male/female difference. In the previous chapter, on women's issues, you'll notice that we specifically focused on "women's needs." In this chapter, you'll notice our language regards "men's issues." Why the difference?

We have found that the word *needs* works better with women, less so with men. Many male executives shut down or just don't open up and articulate when asked, "What are your needs?" They hear this as "female" language, or just don't get a neural resonance with the word. They find it easier to identify *issues they face*. We theorize that the word *issues* works better than *needs* for men because it allows for puzzle solving rather than immediately jumping to emotional content. For males, the route to emotional content is often circuitous. Males, especially busy and powerful male leaders, can turn off from feeling dialogue if it is the lead-in dialogue; puzzle- and problem-solving language is a better lead-in.

In our surveys, we have asked CEOs to tell us the issues men face in their corporations. Male issues that corporations and CEOs have listed include the following, submitted by both male and female leaders. They tend to fit in three categories:

1. Treatment of men by women in the workplace
2. Male life/work balance issues
3. Lack of assistance in learning how to work well with women

Treatment of Men by Women in the Workplace

Men need more respect from women for who men are. Men report experiencing

- Male bashing (men's behavior hated by women or men disliked for being men)
- Pathologizing of men for who they are (through misunderstanding of gender differences)

- A severe pendulum swing in behavioral expectations between genders—expectation that now men must change to become more like women

Male Life/Work Balance Issues

Men report experiencing

- Lack of adequate paternity leave policies or not being empowered to take full advantage of the policy
- Inadequate sick leave to care for children, or taking on the workload when women leave for family emergencies
- Inadequate time and training to be mentored and to mentor others

Lack of Assistance in Learning How to Work Well with Women

Men report experiencing

- Substantial confusion about how to act around women
- Inadequate coaching in understanding and communicating with women
- Inadequate articulation abilities (including words for apology) when males make mistakes that are seen as antifemale aggression but are mainly confusion

---

Try This
A State of Males Questionnaire

Take a moment to journal or just think about whether any of the issues just listed are occurring right now in your workplace. Take a moment with your leadership team, even if just for fairness of gender dialogue, to discuss the issues and those you identified in the exercise "Identify Challenges Men Face" on page 168. If you are a man and you want to bring up in discussion an issue from your own work life, make sure to use particular examples. "I feel bashed" is generally not enough to prove your case. Discussion of male issues needs to take place with clear sensitivity to the fact that in many workplaces many women are still experiencing difficult women's issues.

After successfully moving into a discussion in your close leadership team, move forward to draft a questionnaire that will be sent throughout your corporation. Ask the men and women in your division for anonymous responses. Ask men to describe, in one sentence or paragraph, issues they've faced. List the three categories we just provided, if you wish. Ask the survey participants to be specific on details (though not to use names). Simultaneously, do the same as you ask the women in the corporation to describe issues they have seen men face. Women are often very articulate about issues men have faced. Hear from both men and women, and collate the responses. In your next team meeting, look carefully at the results and develop next steps for action in your corporation.

Men Need Work/Life Balance

An often unsung area of male difficulty is that of parental leave. Women's need to care for children is often assumed (though it can lead to glass ceilings for women), but men's needs for work/child-rearing balance are often misunderstood. Although fewer men than women leave the workplace when they have children—thus less talent is statistically lost—it is important to note the reality of men's biology once they become fathers. As we deal urgently with the loss of moms' talents, we need to look at dads'—gender balance gains from this. Often, corporations are unaware of changes in male biology when the baby comes, and new male needs when men become fathers.

A man's biology changes when he has a child. A Princeton University study recently showed that men's prefrontal cortices (the judging, thinking, executive decision-making part of the brain) develop more synapses and connections after the baby is born—the man becomes more wise, more focused on good decisions, on calming down, paying attention, staying on task.

A man's hormones also change. His oxytocin levels—his bonding chemicals—increase, bonding him to his child. His testosterone levels can diminish (though they can rise again soon, depending on his age). His vasopressin levels can rise (this is a territoriality chemical as well as a bonding vehicle).

When we see men working even harder than before in their professions after having a baby, we may very well be seeing a more focused male brain, expanding its territory and scope of success, in order to fulfill a bond with his child or children—caring for the children, protecting them, caring for his wife and protecting her, all through his hard work.

When we hear men asking for more paternity leave, we are also seeing nature at work. The male brain and its biochemistry makes men hungry to spend more time with family. The birth of children has increased that hunger.

It is crucial to our species that men bond with their offspring during the first months and years of life—bonded fathers are more likely to help adolescents through to adulthood, which in turn creates a better adult, more capable of expressing life vision and finding success, and more helpful (and less dangerous) to the society.

Just as women need help developing part-time options in order for our corporations to retain their talent, so do men. Luckily, some corporations are exploring these options right now and gaining rather than losing financial success. Although not long ago it was unthinkable that an executive would be anything other than a full-time employee, now there are an increasing number of executives who have struck deals with their organizations allowing them to work part-time.

In one accounting firm we worked with, a woman negotiated to go to 80 percent of full-time hours when she had her first child. A male partner who had resigned once he had his first child was recruited back by the company. Its executive team saw how well the part-time option worked for the woman and so made the man a deal to work part-time as well.

This company realized that work/life balance is no longer just a women's issue. It is also a men's issue, and executive flexibility retains both male and female talent. This company did not make these deals with these executives in a vacuum, nor did it countenance losing money. I learned about new studies that show part-timers who work 50 percent of the time actually achieve 70 percent as much work as full-timers. These studies also show that part-time executives bring more reflective thinking into an organization. They have time to reflect and process what is going on.

As part-time options for executives increase, job sharing becomes a reality not just for women but also for men. Xerox recently constructed two mixed executive teams that met the needs of a major client through job sharing. IBM similarly constructed a job share on a major banking client. In IBM's case we met the client, a CIO, who said "I don't know how they do it, but I get better service from that job-share team than I do when the job isn't being shared."

Work/life balance is a common phrase; we use it in this book. Although it is useful, it is also something of a trap. Trying to get work/life balance day after day can be a setup for failure. As any leader knows, there are times when work/life balance must go out the window. If you are closing a big deal, preparing for year-end reviews, or working on a project that requires extensive traveling, for the duration you do not have a balanced life!

Work/life harmony can be a more useful reframing of what is actually happening in your life. Work/life harmony emphasizes that over the course of the year you achieve a reasonable harmony between time at work and time at home. If you know that preparing budgets is going to require late nights next month, you take some time off this month. Gender-intelligent corporations are beginning to give this kind of flexibility to their staff, both male and female. We hope that each executive provided this option will grab it!

For Women: Tips for Supervising Men

We'll end this chapter with scenarios that include common errors some female supervisors make when supervising men. You'll see how inadvertent the errors are, and how wired into male/female brain difference. You'll also see practical solutions. We thank Kathy Stevens, coauthor with Michael Gurian of the *Leading Partners* workbook (2005), for honing these very handy tools. The counterpoint of this tool (tips for men supervising women) appears in Chapter Ten.

Supervising a Man Who Is Angry

A male member of your staff comes into your office and starts venting his frustration about an incident that occurred during his day. He's obviously frustrated. He shares that he is tired of the complaining by some members of his team, annoyed that they aren't meeting deadlines, and on and on.

Trying to be supportive, you respond by empathizing: "I can see how frustrated you are with this situation—let's get it off your chest. Have some coffee, tell me how you're feeling. . . ."

Don't be surprised if the man says, "I don't need a cup of coffee—I need to know what to do about this!"

Your emotive, processing style may not be what your male staff member is looking for at this moment of frustration—he wants solutions, he wants strategies. His task-focused male brain may want to resolve this situation and move on to completing the tasks. He may not see emotional processing as a way to get himself positioned effectively back into the larger system.

A more effective response could be to immediately offer action steps. "Let's make notes about strategies you've tried that don't seem to be working. Then let's make a list of alternatives that you can implement right away." As you take these action steps with him, if you want to pursue emotional content and feeling talk, the most effective approach may be asking how he feels about the system, whether he feels it is breaking down, how he feels the breakdowns can be managed. He may talk about feelings more if they are not about his own internal feelings, but rather about how he and you and everyone else might fit into the effective continuation of a strong system.

At Performance Review Time

Now let's say you are a female supervisor given the task of providing the annual performance review for "Ralph." Ralph has completed nine great projects and had one major mess-up.

Perhaps you begin the session by asking Ralph how the wife and kids are. Did they enjoy their vacation to Yellowstone? How's his mom recovering from her stroke? Perhaps you're trying to show that you care about Ralph. If, however, you see Ralph squirming in his chair or nonverbally signaling discomfort in some other way, you may not be most effectively communicating with him.

Ralph probably wants to know as quickly as possible from you where he stands in the company hierarchy of risk and achievement. He will respect you more if you acknowledge his good work, then get to the point. He will want to know exactly how he messed up (and both asking him and telling him can be important). Then he will probably want to know what resources he needs to make sure he can successfully handle a similar project in the future.

If Ralph says things like, "This mess-up wasn't my fault; it was Joe's (or Sarah's)," you may feel the instinct to engage him on this point with a complex back-and-forth, beginning with "Why do you say that?" and going into great detail for half an hour. This may be necessary, and only you can decide what is best, but it is also worth remembering that this blaming-another exercise may just be a quick defensive response (Ralph trying to keep his own status intact); it is a common male defensive response, and it may well dissipate on its own within minutes of your helping him do a better job in the future.

Overall, when men mess something up, they need supervisors to help them return toward supportive goal-oriented procedures for redress and new work. They need supervisors to not get caught up in competitive mechanisms, but instead keep them focused on outcomes;

and they often want to be successful under their own power as soon as possible; that is, returning to the position on the project that allows them to earn esteem in the company again through efforts and resolve—as an individual or part of the team.

For men, process may not be as important as goal and product, and this difference may well be a lighthouse for women supervisors that never moves, never goes away, and needs to be factored into managerial roles of women. Quite often, if a woman can listen to a male supervisee and hear, behind all the other words, these words: *Help me solve this problem so I can retain my respect and status, or even advance it,* she will engage with men in a way that is not only gender intelligent, but also furthers her own and other women's passion to achieve gender balance in an organization. Men who are respected for who they are become very powerful allies indeed.

Bringing It All Together: A Final GenderTool

We have ended this chapter with a helpful set of scenarios and practical strategies involving management and supervision of talent. This "supervisor's notebook" is not only gender friendly on its own, but also a transition to the last GenderTool and last chapter of this book: our chapter on gender mentoring and coaching. As we've progressed in helping you build your gender intelligence and maneuver your team toward greater gender balance, we've tried to provide you with analysis, applications, and tools that help you as an individual to expand your authenticity as a woman or man. Our ultimate goal is to bring gender intelligence and gender balance to you as a next step in authentic leadership development.

In no part of corporate life is it possible to fully maximize human potential and natural gender assets without mentoring and coaching. We cannot be fully authentic unless we both receive mentoring and become gender-intelligent mentors ourselves. We gain whole selves and authentic power by learning from masters around us, and we give back the power and self to others by becoming, for them, masters who can help them reach their authentic potential.

In the gender arena, men and women need men and women as gender-intelligent mentors. As you move toward the conclusion of this book, we hope you will find the final GenderTool a useful way of applying this book's material toward a fully restructured and evolved team and corporation.

Situational Exercise

In your team discussion, consider three issues for males in your corporation and write them down. Pay particular attention, if appropriate, to the amount of male bashing in your corporation. Make sure, even if you can't develop policy in your corporation for all the issues raised here, that you at least work on policy for that one.

Fifth Principle and Task of Balanced Leadership

Principle 5: When we apply science-based insight about gender, we alter our corporate vision to fully understand men and what they need in the workplace. Men bring immense strengths to the gender dialogue, and they also bring specific issues that are part of the gender evolution in contemporary business.

Task/Actions 5: Apply gender science to your workplace with men in mind. Survey your workforce to figure out men's strengths and issues. Supervise men in ways that are specifically effective for them.

Summary

1. Gender balance requires us to look carefully at men's perspectives, issues, and inherent strengths.
2. Sometimes men's issues get lost in our development of female-friendly frameworks, leading to many men "checking out" of helping with women's issues.

3. Men bring a primal difference from women to the workplace regarding how they build self-esteem in others and themselves.
4. Men experience male bashing that leads to loss of male talent.
5. Many men in the workforce want help working with women on a daily basis.
6. Family leave issues are not fully addressed for men in our workplaces.
7. Women's supervisory skills are most effective with men when they include gender intelligence frameworks.

GenderTool 5

Practicing Gender-Intelligent Mentoring and Coaching in Your Corporation

A good business leader doesn't just lead a business. A good leader is also a mentor to people on a daily basis.

—DAVE ROTH, FORMER VP/ENGINEERING, VIVATO SYSTEMS

THE PHYSICIAN ALBERT SCHWEITZER PAID HOMAGE TO THE MENTORS who helped him be successful. "At times," he said, "our own light goes out and is rekindled by a spark from another person. Each of us has cause to think with deep gratitude of those who have lighted the flame within us." As each of us does at various times in our lives, he sensed his own deep need for assistance on the human journey. He was mentored when he needed mentoring, and he became a mentor to others as they needed him to be.

Few endeavors are more important in the work of gender intelligence and gender balance than *mentoring* (in this chapter we will generally use this term to include coaching and elements of supervision as well). Men and women need one another to help them become more successful. The gender evolution in our new millennium will gradually expand the role of the mentor. It is already doing so, in many ways. We know that authentic leadership is not fully possible without mentoring and coaching—none of us can lead alone. In the area of gender, this is especially true. We can look into the future and say that we will have achieved full gender balance in leadership when

- Women have the female mentors they need
- Women have the male mentors they need
- Men have the male mentors they need
- Men have the female mentors they need

Research over the last twenty years has consistently found mentoring to be one of the key factors in retention of talent. *Power Mentoring*, by Ellen Ensher and Susan Murphy, is a very useful read on this research. The hidden everyday experiences of leadership, the inner battles, the competition and conflicts, the enjoyment and stress are all more likely to lead to success when we are mentored and mentor others. Research from both academic studies and within corporations shows that when the full potential for mentoring is not realized in a corporation, women cannot advance and be retained to the extent the corporation needs. Men, too, need other men and other women to mentor them in developing their own authentic leadership skills as men. Mentoring is by no means for women only. It is especially useful to keep in mind the bottom-line value of mentoring. When a manager or partner is not retained, the cost is high. For a white-collar middle manager, for instance, the cost is about $100,000—this includes costs of recruitment, training, and lost productivity. The higher up the manager is in the hierarchy, the higher the costs.

Corporate research over the last two decades demonstrates that mentored individuals advance more rapidly in an organization, earn higher salaries, are less likely to leave the organization, and express more favorable work attitudes than individuals who are not mentored. Mentoring programs really work. At Best Buy, for instance, the company realized that women influence 80 percent of electronics purchases and spent $68 billion on electronics per year. Best Buy wanted to recruit women into leadership in order to figure out how to fully tap into women's buying power. It was a very male-dominated culture, with the turnover rate of females double that of males. Best Buy developed a mentoring and networking program to help female employees. Retention of women immediately increased. Best Buy was assisted by the Women's Leadership Forum (WOLF), which innovates in this area.

Deloitte & Touche similarly succeeded in using mentoring and coaching to help build up their bottom line. As they included gender intelligence training for all their partners, they simultaneously created mentoring systems for both women and men. The importance of this next step (including men in the mentoring efforts) was crucial. Paul Silverglate, a leader of the company's Women's Initiative (WIN), has remarked, "If you really want to make a difference for women, it has to make sense for all the partners." Paying attention to men's mentoring and coaching needs helped women, just as paying attention to women's mentoring and coaching needs helped men.

Tom Anderson, CFO and vice president of CSG, Inc., recently summed up the research on mentoring when he told Michael, "Whether you are a man or a woman, you just don't feel confident sometimes to pursue opportunities, especially risky ones, if you don't have a mentor who helps you see whether you are being authentic to who you are and want to be." In the end, this is what mentoring is all about. Each of us wants to make a journey through work and life in which we gain insight into who we are and want to be, and we want help bringing this authentic self into relationship with others—coworkers, bosses, employees, customers.

The Importance of Mentoring and Coaching in Gender Science

Mentoring is important not only from a research and intuitive point of view, but also from a scientific gender perspective. Researchers Beverly Kaye and Sharon Jordan-Evans recently compiled a survey of fifteen thousand employees in many industries. They asked them what drives employee retention. For both women and men, the top five drivers—exciting work, career growth, good relationships, fair pay, and good bosses—were affected by how well the employees were led and mentored.

The research on oxytocin levels in women that we discussed earlier gives clues to the women's internal need for mentoring in the areas of workplace comfort and retention. Women often report feeling more comfortable and productive when they are connecting with someone to work on an issue, look at a design, produce a presentation, or lead a meeting. One woman executive told us, "I'm a pretty tough woman—some would say I lean more toward your bridge brain or even third sex kind of woman—but even I need people around me. I need to be relating, talking, connecting. When I first started out, I didn't have any mentoring, and the feeling of aloneness made me leave that company."

This female executive still feels—even in our enlightened era—that she'll be considered weak for expressing her need. Her expression of it, however, is a necessary part of the gender evolution. This woman may indeed have the higher testosterone of many male and female leaders. Research over the last decade, most recently by Helen Fisher, has shown that many of the highest-level female executives have higher-than-average testosterone levels. (Fisher wonders: Is it because they were born that way? Is it because leading a big corporation is competitive and thus stimulates the aggression chemical, testosterone?) These women will also have higher oxytocin levels than the men around them. Thus, to feel connected and in control they will most likely need the support of emotional bonds that endure through and in spite of the competition.

Looking on the male side, biological sciences have been curious for decades about the biological origins of male mentoring systems. The most obvious biological cause of the male's constant need for mentoring (think of the father's influence on a boy, the adolescent's need for strong coaches and teachers who take a special interest in helping him develop into a moral, compassionate, and competent man) may well come from the male's high level of testosterone.

Once males hit puberty, their testosterone levels surge for many years. They become more physically and socially aggressive (even shy males become relatively more aggressive). As we've discussed, this is an adaptive and functional aspect of the male gender that can provide them with the career-advancing, risk-taking, undistracted task focus, but this same internal drive needs help in finding appropriate channels for its energy: motivational assistance, direction toward purpose and service, and help finding a sense of self and ways of building serenity and balance into male life. Human societies have always provided mentors for males as a primal way of helping them focus on where to direct their energy, how to develop their skills and craft, and how to successfully navigate human relationships with both women and men.

Mentoring is also crucial for helping men to develop their verbal skills. Males often misread verbal signals from others, especially in complex psychosocial settings like the workplace; they particularly often misread the verbalizations of women. Mentoring for males, especially aggressive ones or ones who don't understand women, can make the difference between success and failure at work.

GenderTool 5: Focusing on Mentoring and Coaching

At the beginning of this book we described gender with the metaphor of a lighthouse. It is constantly giving off light that we can use to guide us toward success for women and men. In the same vein, we quoted Albert Schweitzer at the beginning of this chapter. Mentoring of women and men—helping both sexes to learn about and value gender differences through direct contact with women and men who can coach them on how to act—is a direct and rewarding exploitation of the light constantly available to us. We hope that as you finish this book you will be able to become a mentor to one or more women and men. We hope you will have gained from us essential information for your journey not only as an individual who may need help within a company to succeed to your authentic potential, but also as an individual who can now help other men and women.

To help you and your team, we've created this fifth GenderTool. We thank gender marketing expert Katherine Coles, a coauthor with Michael of *The Leading Partners Workbook,* for her contributions. Every component of this tool is based on field-tested research in corporations.

Mentoring Happens in Three Primary Areas

When mentoring women and men, three primary areas of focus emerge, with each quite often handled differently depending on whether the mentor is helping a woman or man:

- *Career support.* The individual being mentored—the mentee—needs help with specific career track issues; for example, advancement up a leadership ladder.
- *Psychosocial support.* The mentee needs a listening ear for relational issues, help dealing with a particular leader, help dealing with a crisis at work or elsewhere.
- *Gender intelligence support.* The mentee needs help understanding the other gender's signals and developing a plan for action in relation to the other gender.

Situational Exercise

Do You Need Mentoring?

Being mentored is natural to us, yet it is not easy to ask for mentoring, and often we don't realize we need it.

Take a moment to look at the three primary focus areas we just listed. Then get out three blank sheets of paper.

Now think about whether you need the first kind of mentoring, career support. If so, on the first sheet write down why. Use a bullet list to note separate incidents with other people or corporations. Look back at previous places you've worked. Do you see any patterns? For instance, did you need mentoring in a past place of employment but didn't get it?

Think about whether you need mentoring in the second area, psychosocial support. Using the same method, write down why on the second sheet.

Think about whether you need help in the third area, gender intelligence support. Write down why on the third sheet.

Talk to others you trust about your answers to these questions. If you can see that you need mentoring, who can you ask for the mentoring?

If career support is your area of vulnerability, is there someone in your corporation now who can help you—someone above you in the hierarchy or someone who is a powerful peer? Is there a mentoring system available through the human resources department? Is there an executive coach available to you?

If psychosocial support is your area of need, do you have a trustworthy friend in the corporation—someone who listens, understands, and can also direct you to resources?

If gender intelligence is your area of difficulty, what man or woman can help you understand how the other gender works, thinks, behaves?

Finding the right mentor can be a career-saving step. Get all the help you can, and if you can't get the help in-house, rely on external executive coaches who keep confidentiality.

Situational Exercise

Becoming a Mentor

Someone around you right now needs your help. It's as simple as that. Someone is having career difficulty, psychosocial difficulty, gender difficulty. Or some woman or man may be having no specific difficulty right now, but may just be a wonderful, talented young woman or man who needs you to bring your light and flame to their work and their ambition so that they can flourish.

Take a moment to think about who this person or persons might be. As you did in the preceding exercise, get out a sheet of paper.

Do you know someone, male or female, who needs career support from you? Write that name down. Think about how to approach this person and offer help. Think about what you think this person needs. Write notes to yourself for later use.

Do you know someone, male or female, who needs relational, social, or personal guidance from you? Write that name down and explore the same thoughts.

Do you know someone who needs help understanding and working with the other gender? Follow the same steps.

When you can, take the risk of offering help to these individuals. You can't know the outcome of that risk ahead of time, or the readiness of the person to accept help, but you can try to offer what light you have to give.

For Mentors: A Checklist

If and when you do become a mentor to the person or persons you identified in the preceding exercise, here is a brief checklist for career support that can help you ascertain how you are doing. If you are already a mentor, this checklist can provide a constructive framework for areas of need that may still exist.

To-Do Checklist:

- ❏ Provide in-house sponsoring of your mentee that provides visibility, credibility, legitimacy.
- ❏ Provide your mentee with access to some or all of your own success network.
- ❏ Provide your mentee with coaching on how to negotiate his or her advancement in relationships with others in the corporation.
- ❏ Provide your mentee with specific and challenging assignments that give preparation, visibility, and credibility for advancement.
- ❏ Help your mentee get noticed for special assignments within the organization.

❑ Advise your mentee on how to get promoted and educate her or him on promotion criteria.

❑ Keep your mentee focused on doing the right work and the highest-quality work—the work that leads to success.

❑ Teach your mentee how to deal with nuances of the worker-boss relationship from the boss's perspective.

❑ Teach your mentee how to create his or her own network to push projects forward.

❑ Teach your mentee how to interact with the high-level executives in *your* corporation.

Mentoring Women

Here are the most frequently reported gender challenges women list when asked what they need mentoring on. These coincide with the three focus areas already described. Focusing on them can deepen your assistance to women in each area.

- Removing gender barriers
- Navigating the traditional male hierarchies
- Increasing access to informal networks
- Increasing visibility of female role models
- Building legitimacy and credibility in order to advance in management
- Learning the ropes and dealing with the environment for advancement
- Being mentored by women
- Being mentored by men

Practical Strategies: Mentoring Women Toward Success

Mentoring and being mentored can be a risky and humbling experience. As women seek out and accept mentoring from both women and men, and as, concomitantly, both women and men provide the mentoring, all parties must expect some discomfort at some point. Here are specific actions that often must be taken to fully mentor women.

WHEN IMPORTANT CLIENTS PREFER THE MALE EXECUTIVE   Sometimes important clients have the view that female leaders will not be a perfect fit and that having a woman lead the project will hurt the business relationship. As one male leader revealed, in reporting his mentoring efforts: "I've experienced clients saying to me that they really want a male executive on their project. I find I have to push back and tell them that the woman is the best candidate and has outstanding skills. The client realizes I'm sort of her 'rabbi,' and must know what I'm doing, and accepts the woman onto the project. Then, when she works out well, everyone is happy. My job as a mentor is to push for her to get the job. If I didn't push, she wouldn't get the job. In another generation or so, this might not be needed—I don't know—but right now, it is needed, and I have to be ready to help her in this way."

WHEN A WOMAN IS SLOWER THAN A MAN TO SAY "YES" TO A PROJECT   Male leaders report that when they offer an opportunity to a female leader she sometimes seems more hesitant in leaping at it than a man would be. What leaders are saying is that quite often men will go for it even if they only have a sketchy idea of what is involved; equally qualified women may want more information and seek more certainty. It leads men to wonder whether the woman really wants the opportunity or not. Mentors play a crucial role here, in insisting that the qualified woman look closely at the new job, providing her with the information she needs, and being patient with her style of choice making. She can be given a deadline like anyone else, but she may need some extra time, and that can work out quite well in the end.

WHEN WOMEN DON'T BLOW THEIR OWN HORNS   Both women and men report that women don't blow their own horns within the leadership team. The simple act of making sure people know your achievements can advance a career, and women may need help from mentors in developing both overt and subtle ways to blow their own horns. If a qualified and high-achieving woman seems too cautious about self-promotion, you may need to help her develop this skill. You may need to get her in a room with the person she needs to talk to about her successes and skills. You may need to coach her in what words to use and how to talk about herself and her successes.

WHEN A WOMAN IS NOT BEING DIRECT ENOUGH   Both male and female leaders report that many very talented women choose, by their nature, an indirect style of relationship: these women need to relate to very direct, high-achieving men who "don't like to waste time" and who also perceive that these women constantly "waste their time" by beating around the bush, not giving the real story, lacking candor. Women in this situation need both female and male mentors to help them learn how to develop frankness that leads to specific solutions. This kind of candor will actually get them quite far with male leaders—and developing it, through mentoring and coaching, does not require a woman to become the third sex.

For Men: Tips for Supervising Women

In Chapter Nine we shared with women a tool for supervision that included tips for supervising male employees. If you are a man who supervises or manages women, you are in a mentoring position with the other gender. In two cases in particular, you as a man may find yourself needing to pay close attention to what you've learned about gender intelligence:

- During times of stress in an employee's or colleague's workday, when the supervisor is called on to help process or problem-solve
- At performance review time

The practical scenarios we offer here are composites of the kind of adjustment that male mentors—specifically supervisors—can and need to make to effectively mentor the female relating style.

During a Time of Stress

A female member of your staff comes into your office and starts sharing her frustration about an incident that occurred during her day. She's obviously angry and using a lot of words to voice that feeling. She shares that she is tired of the complaining by some members of her team, annoyed that they aren't meeting deadlines, and so on. Trying to be helpful, you immediately begin making suggestions on how to deal with the situation.

She stops and looks at you—now she's obviously frustrated with you! You don't enjoy her reaction, as you were trying to help her. In your mind, you "got what she was saying" after a minute of talk, and now it's time to task focus, problem solve, and get to bottom-line thinking.

You may be missing the fact that, especially in a moment of stress, you and she are wired differently. She is wired to process her frustrations through words and, through this experience, come to internal conclusions (and get support). She didn't need you to solve her problem; she just needed you to listen, show empathy, and give her feelings importance and relevance. What can you do the next time a situation like this occurs?

When she walks into your office and starts sharing her frustrations, you can say, "Let me be sure of what you need from me—do you need me to help you solve a problem or do you just need me to listen?" If she says she just needs you to listen, do just that! Listen attentively—reflect some of what you hear so she knows you understand, and don't start problem solving unless she asks you to!

At Performance Review Time

Let's say you are the male supervisor responsible for annual performance reviews of a female staff member. During the past year this staff member, "Jenny," has been assigned ten projects. She successfully completed nine of them on time, under budget, and generally did a great job. But assignment ten was different—it just didn't work out.

Jenny comes into your office and sits down. You begin with "Jenny, what happened to this project? It really didn't work."

Jenny looks at you, and in her mind she's thinking, "I did nine projects perfectly, and all he can focus on is the one that had problems. I am absolutely not valued by this company." She's feeling really disheartened, and won't hear much of what you have to say after that.

This might work much better:

"Jenny, I'm really pleased and impressed with your work on projects one through nine this year. You showed a lot of initiative and represented the company like a champion. What was different on project ten? It just didn't click—what needed to happen to make it as successful as the other nine? How could we have helped?"

You have shown appreciation, acknowledged the staff member for her good work, and become a partner in helping her work through the problem project. You have opened the door for her to come to you for help when she's stuck, knowing you are supportive.

Mentoring Men

Here are the most frequently reported gender challenges men list when asked what they need mentoring on:

- Removing barriers to advancement
- Understanding and navigating female ways of relating
- Feeling left out of female conversations
- Feeling gossiped about
- Walking on eggshells with women
- Needing a male mentor to help them advance
- Needing help with work/life balance issues
- Wanting help from both men and women

Practical Strategies: Mentoring Men Toward Success

Because of our focus in corporations today on the retention and advancement of women, and because we know that female role models and mentoring of women is so crucial, we can often focus so much on women's mentoring that we neglect to pay close attention to men's needs for mentoring. As men seek out and accept mentoring from both women and men, and as, concomitantly, both women and men provide the mentoring, specific actions can be taken by both genders to fully mentor men.

WHEN A MAN NEEDS CAREER HELP   Men often do not ask for the help they need, yet they often need a mentor to help them advance. When we worked with the Los Angeles Police Department, internal networks for helping men advance were quite clear. Men helped younger men. In some Fortune 500 companies we've worked with, there is more confusion. Sometimes both women and men who lead are so busy they forget to mentor younger men. Male talent can get lost if a man (especially a shy, quiet man who won't ask for help) falls through the cracks. You can become a mentor to this man.

WHEN A MAN DOESN'T KNOW HOW TO GIVE WOMEN FEEDBACK Men often need mentoring on how to give feedback, both to men and to women. We were at a talent management committee meeting for a financial institution. The committee was ready to dismiss a certain woman SVP because she hadn't shown sufficient strategic thinking. When we spoke to her later we learned she had no idea there was negativity about her. We met with her boss in a private meeting, and he said, "Well, I've alluded to it, but she hasn't picked up on it." We asked the obvious question: "Yes, but have you told her?" He skated around that for a while before drifting into the explanation that "I'm not sure how she would take it." This man didn't know how to give a woman feedback. He soft-pedaled her or didn't provide any feedback at all. The corporation was about to lose her talent. The male boss was not malicious; in fact, he was trying to protect this woman by not hurting her feelings. This is an area of contact between female and male leaders in which mentoring and coaching is crucial for men.

PRACTICAL IDEAS FOR GIVING FEEDBACK TO A FEMALE LEADER If you are mentoring or coaching a man who is having trouble giving feedback to a female leader, help him focus on

- Asking open-ended questions that create dialogue
- Complimenting specific achievement outcomes
- Asking for feedback on why something went wrong, rather than just telling the woman his opinion of what she did wrong
- Using positive reinforcement that frames negative outcomes in actionable next steps—don't blame, just move forward

Try This
Use the Declare–Frame–Check Approach

Both women and men can gain from being constantly mentored in good communication and feedback skills. If you are working with a mentee who is having trouble giving feedback, mentor him (or her) in this quick tool:

1. *Declare* your intention: "I want to help you by giving positive feedback on what is going well and then pointing out an area to improve."

2. *Frame* the situation: "I think the project went well in these specific areas" (list and note them in whatever detail is necessary). After engaging with the other person in the details and asking questions like "What do you think went well?" the mentee can frame the improvements he wants in the context of the positive achievements.

3. *Check* that the other person understands intention with questions and dialogue: "Does what I'm saying make sense?" After engaging in this dialogue, ask for action steps, listen to them, and give feedback on which ones seem most fruitful.

WHEN A MAN NEEDS HELP WITH WORK/LIFE BALANCE   Our research consistently shows a need among men to get help in developing work/life balance. Many male executives in particular find their work addictive. They feel as if they literally pulse with the biochemical and social energy to conquer and succeed. They work in the office, they bring their work home. Often, lacking appropriate mentoring within their corporations, they don't see alternatives. A mentor who helps them develop work/life balance can become a kind of lifeline for these men. This mentor can be a woman (or more than one person), but sometimes the best choice is an older man who has already been there and can give both logistical and relational wisdom on how to give equally to both work and family.

Make Mentoring a Part of Your Corporation's Infrastructure

In this GenderTool we are providing specific and individual advice on how to mentor. Although mentoring can and must be done individually, in order for mentors and mentees to be fully supported, mentoring programs must be inculcated into large corporations. You'll need resources (financial and personnel) to create a mentoring system such that lasts and helps your corporation. Here is a checklist of essential components:

- ❏ *A task force.* Generally, you need a task force in place to make sure you have identified primary and secondary areas in which mentoring is especially needed in your corporation; for example, gender relationships, racial diversity, developing young talent, mentoring women, mentoring men. The task force will definitely gain from being gender-balanced.
- ❏ *Diagnostics and a plan.* In the area of gender specifically, executive coaches who specialize in gender can help diagnose issues and develop a mentoring plan. Each company is different from other companies, thus there is no "one plan fits all."
- ❏ *Training.* Mentoring works best, especially in the first year, when it is accompanied by professional development opportunities in-house. Individuals often need training in how to mentor, especially in gender intelligence and specifically mentoring of women and men.
- ❏ *Promulgation of executive buy-in.* As mentoring takes hold in a corporation, it is crucial that executive buy-in is promulgated in-house. All managerial levels need to know that mentoring and an in-house mentoring program are priorities.

Generally speaking, if your corporation decides to focus on mentoring programs and adequately prepares itself through personnel, diagnostics, planning, training, and buy-in, the mentoring program can become a pivot point for improvement in talent retention rates as well as greater workplace comfort and productivity for men.

Training Mentors

Not everyone feels that mentoring is natural to them. Sometimes you will have to teach skills or arrange for someone else to teach mentoring skills to individual mentors. This skill building can keep a mentoring program stable and useful.

It's especially useful to teach potential mentors how to

- Ascertain the various kinds of mentoring that can assist mentees
- Develop a comprehensive network of support that is a fit for the individual mentee
- Deal with ambiguities in relationships without blaming others or oneself
- Use any online tools the organization has that support mentor processes
- Coach people through mistakes and avoid finding scapegoats
- Communicate most effectively (and differently as needed) with various individuals in power positions
- Coach people to develop their credibility in the leadership team
- Be honest about one's own flaws and change flawed behavior

Try This
An Exercise for Your Leadership Team

Your company has created a formal mentoring program. At the end of the first year, you want to conduct an evaluation of the program based on reports provided by both mentors and mentees.

What are some of the comments the company should see to indicate whether the program has been successful? Write your answers on a blank sheet of paper.

Example:

- My mentor provided me with advice that would have taken me years to learn on my own.
- My mentor introduced me to other individuals who have helped my career.
- My mentee was successful in completing assignments that he or she initially didn't believe could be accomplished.

Mentoring for the New Millennium

There are a number of very powerful mentoring programs in today's corporations, but many are a standardized, one-size-fits-all approach, and many do not emphasize what this book has emphasized: the importance of understanding and supporting human nature's role in male and female authentic leadership.

Our research shows that some women enter these programs only to find they are being coached to change to a male leadership approach. Men, on the other hand, find they are only or mainly coached on how to help women advance through what they perceive to be "soft science" or "touchy-feely" trainings.

Companies that become aware of this problem sometimes decide that they will get women to mentor women—which is crucial but can also leave women feeling even more excluded from male networks. Also, many Gen X and Y women report to us that some female mentors grew up in a very different world—some of their advice comes from old frames not suitable to the current workplace and the young women's aspirations. Overreliance on women mentoring women can be difficult as well because of the dearth of senior women available to be mentors. One female leader told us she had been assigned to mentor eight women—on top of what was more than a full-time job already! She felt guilty, like she was doing a poor job of mentoring, and didn't know what to do for everyone.

Female mentors are as crucial for women as male mentors are crucial for men, but so, too, is cross-gender mentoring. The mentoring programs of the future will move in the direction of providing both women and men to mentor both women and men. The act of mentoring, and the experience of supervising and coaching, are immensely rewarding for leaders—these are soulful acts, unforgettable, emotionally powerful, deeply touching. The experience of being mentored is equally soulful, and we crave it, whether from a woman or a man.

As you near the end of this book, we hope that you, in your executive team, will discuss what you as an executive and managerial group can do to create or improve your mentoring program. We hope you'll go around the boardroom for just a moment and talk about who your mentors were when you grew up, then while you were in college or your first jobs, then more recently, as you advanced into your present position. Remember aloud with your colleagues who coached you, cared about you, saw the light and flame in you and nurtured it.

Many of the issues women and men have faced in any work environment in the past have not been solvable without a mentoring component in place. The same holds true in your present corporation. To mentor and be mentored is a part of our human DNA. As you are mentored and mentor others, you are participating in a profoundly important part of being a woman or a man.

EPILOGUE: THE FUTURE OF GENDER

People say, "It's only the journey that matters, not the destination."
In business, they both matter. You have to enjoy the journey, but if
you don't get to the destination, someone else will—and you'll be
out of luck.

—GENE DIRE, CORPORATE TRAINER, CERTIFIED BY KEN BLANCHARD COMPANIES

WHEN THE TRADITIONALIST FRAME RULED THE GENDER conversation in
various cultures (for much of our history), the conversation was
about survival through gender limitations. When the feminist frame
emerged into the conversation, it became about both survival and
new freedom for women. We hope you've found, through tools like
this book and the people you've met in it—and ultimately through
your own gender work—that the nature-based and science-based gender frame stimulates a conversation between women and men that is
still (and always) about survival, definitely about freedom for women,
and now, also, about long-lasting partnership for men and women who
want to be authentic leaders, as women and men.

Human nature is and always has been the prime mover of our
instincts, and our workplaces are instinctual places filled with ambition, power, and need. The new gender evolution combines instinct
with passion and passion with reason. The ultimate destination of this

work is to ensure a future of gender relations that can awaken in each of us, and thus in our children—our future leaders and workforce—a deep respect for who we are and they are, why each of us is here and why each of them is here. Newly energized by this respect, corporate leaders of the present and future can take dynamic leadership into the community at large, effecting social change.

The issue before us, as we use science to understand gender, is the issue of life purpose. We and those we care for—as well as our colleagues and our consumers—each want to feel meaningful and purposeful in life. This feeling—profound and very real—is gained in part by our free and reasonable expression as women and men. It has always been this way and always will be.

In this book, you have taken a journey through brain research into gender intelligence and balanced leadership. You've been asked to see your everyday work life through the light of a million years of male and female development. You've been provided with GenderTools to help you do the work of gender intelligence in your leadership team. We hope you've felt that everything provided to you was based not only on scientific inquiry, but also on wisdom of practice in corporations like yours.

This book has been, we hope, a tool for your journey, but it is not the destination. You and the future of your workplace are the destination. You as an individual leader have a great deal of power; your leadership team has even more. We hope this book has helped you and the men and women around you to fulfill your callings as individuals and your collective calling as a team. We hope you will be revolutionary in your gender discussions, reframing, and retooling. Success in terms of bottom lines should be forthcoming from this revolution, and so, too, success as human beings. All doors are now open for us as men and women in partnership. Let's walk through them together.

NOTES AND RESOURCES

INTRODUCTON:

HOW GENDER INTELLIGENCE LEADS
TO BALANCED, AUTHENTIC LEADERSHIP

DID YOU KNOW? A SNAPSHOT OF GENDER DIFFERENCES

Annis, B. *Same Words, Different Language*. New York: Penguin Books, 2004.

Baron-Cohen, S. *The Essential Difference*. New York: Basic Books, 2003.

Brizendine, L., M.D. *The Female Brain*. New York: Broadway Books, 2006.

Carter, R. *Mapping The Mind*. Los Angeles: University of California Press, 1998.

Jessel, D., and A. Moir. *Brain Sex: The Real Difference Between Men and Women*. New York: Dell, 1992.

Onion, A. "Sex in the Brain: Research Showing Men and Women Differ in More Than One Area." *ABC News*, 21 September 2004.

Rhoads, S. E. *Taking Sex Differences Seriously*. San Francisco: Encounter Books, 2004.

Salomone, R. C. *Same, Different, Equal*. New Haven and London: Yale University Press, 2003.

A GENDER PARTNERSHIP

Blanchard, K. and S. Johnson. *The One Minute Manager*. New York: William Morrow, 1984.

Covey, S. *Seven Habits of Highly Effective People*. New York: Free Press, 2004.

Dvorak, P., and J. Badal. "This Is Your Brain on the Job." *Wall Street Journal*, 20 September 2007.

George, B., P. Sims, and D. Gergen. *True North*. San Francisco: Jossey-Bass, Warren Bennis Series, 2007.

Halpern, D. F., C. P. Benbow, D. C. Geary, R. C. Gur, J. S. Hyde, and M. A. Gernsbacher. "The Science of Sex Differences in Science and Mathematics." *Psychological Science in the Public Interest* (August 2007), 8 (1).

Heim, P., and S. Golant. *Hardball for Women*. New York: Plume, 2005.

Hewlett, S. A. *On Ramps, Off Ramps*. Boston: Harvard Business School Press, 2007.

Pearce, T. *Leading Out Loud*. San Francisco: Jossey-Bass, 2003.

Razeghi, A. *Hope*. San Francisco: Jossey-Bass, 2006.

Jeffrey Schwartz and Warren Bennis are quoted in "The Business Brain in Close-Up," *Business Week*, July 21, 2007.

CHAPTER ONE
UNDERSTANDING THE SCIENCE
OF GENDER

Note: Both the Gurian Institute and Barbara Annis and Associates (BAAINC) have, over the last decade, interviewed and spoken with scientists in the gender field, and used their information in books, lectures, and trainings. A number of the brain facts referenced with laboratory studies in these Notes and Resources have been corroborated by the original scientists in personal interviews. These individuals include Daniel Amen, M.D., of the Amen Clinics; Linda Babcock, Ph.D., of Carnegie Mellon; Helen Fisher, Ph.D.; Ruben Gur, Ph.D., of University of Pennsylvania; Marianne Legato, M.D., of Columbia University; Tracey Shors, Ph.D., of Rutgers; and Sandra Witelson, Ph.D., of McMaster University.

Halpern, Benbow, Geary, Gur, Hyde, and Gernsbacher, "The Science of Sex Differences in Science and Mathematics," 2007.

GETTING TO KNOW THE GENDER/BRAIN SPECTRUM

Amen, D., M.D. *Making A Good Brain Great*. New York: Three Rivers Press, 2006.

"Intelligence in Men And Women Is a Gray and White Matter." *ScienceDaily*, 22 January 2005. [www.sciencedaily.com/releases/2005/01/050121100142.htm]

Jessel and Moir. *Brain Sex*, 1992.

Sax, L. *Why Gender Matters*. New York: Doubleday, 2005.

HOW DOES THE BRAIN GET HARD-WIRED
FOR GENDER DIFFERENCES?

Mack, C., R. McGivern, L. Hyde, and V. Denenberg. "Absence of Postnatal Testosterone Fails to Demasculinize the Male Rat's Corpus Callosum." *Developmental Brain Research* (1996), 95: 252–254.

Vilain, E., K. McElreavey, F. Richaud, and M. Fellous. "Isolation of the Sex-Determining Gene in Men." *Pathologie et biologie* (Paris) (1992), 40 (1): 15-7.

CAN THE BRAIN BE REPROGRAMMED FOR GENDER?

Jensen, E. *Enriching the Brain*. San Francisco: Jossey-Bass, 2006.

Kimura, D. "Human Sex Differences in Cognition: Fact, Not Predicament." *Sexualities, Evolution & Gender* (2004), 6: 45–53. Simon Fraser University, BC, Canada.

Wood, W., and A. H. Eagly. "A Cross-Cultural Analysis of the Behavior of Women and Men: Implications for the Origins of Sex Differences." *Psychological Bulletin* (2002), 128 (5): 699–727.

Zhumkhawala, S. "Dolls, Trucks, and Identity." *Children's Advocate* (November–December 1997). Action Alliance for Children, Oakland, CA. [www.4children.org/news/1197doll.htm]

DID YOU KNOW? MALE AND FEMALE TEAR
GLANDS ARE DIFFERENT BY NATURE

Marcozzi, G., V. Liberati, F. Madia, M. Centofanti, and G. de Feo. "Age- and Gender-Related Differences in Human Lacrimal Fluid Peroxidase Activity." *Ophthalmologica* (2003), 217: 294–297 (DOI: 10.1159/000070638).

BURNING QUESTION: ARE THERE EXCEPTIONS
TO THE GENDER RULES?

David Amen, M.D., interview with Michael Gurian, 2006. Brain scans provided by the Amen Clinics. [www.amenclinics.com]

Baron-Cohen. *The Essential Difference*, 2003.

CHAPTER TWO

UNDERSTANDING HOW THE MALE AND
FEMALE BRAIN WORK DIFFERENTLY

BLOOD FLOW PATTERNS IN THE BRAIN

The whole August 2007 issue of *Psychological Science* is devoted to male and female brain differences. The scientists who coauthored the issue are among the top in the field worldwide. The issue touches on nearly every brain difference that is applied in this book. We highly recommend this study.

Halpern, Benbow, Geary, Gur, Hyde, and Gernsbacher. "The Science of Sex Differences in Science and Mathematics," 2007.

Hines, M. "Prenatal Testosterone and Gender-Related Behaviour." *European Journal of Endocrinology* (November 1, 2006), 155 (Suppl. 1): S115–S121.

Knickmeyer, C., and S. Baron-Cohen. "Fetal Testosterone and Sex Differences?" *Early Human Development*, 82 (12): 755–760.

Legato, M., M.D., interview with David Creelman, 2006.

SPATIAL-MECHANICAL AND VERBAL-EMOTIVE DIFFERENCES

Eals, M., and I. Silverman. "The Hunter-Gatherer Theory of Spatial Sex Differences: Proximate Factors Mediating the Female Advantage in Recall of Object Arrays." *Ethology and Sociobiology* (1994), 15: 95–105.

Frederikse, M., A. Lu, E. Aylward, P. Barta, and G. Pearlson. "Sex Differences in the Inferior Parietal Lobule." *Cerebral Cortex* (1999), 9: 896–901.

Gryn, G., A. Wunderlich, M. Spitzer, T. Reinhard, and M. Riepe. "Brain Activation During Human Navigation: Gender-Different Neural Networks as Substrate of Performance." *Nature Neuroscience* (April 2000), 3 (4): 404–408.

Gur, R., et al. "An fMRI Study of Sex Differences in Regional Activation to a Verbal and Spatial Task." *Brain and Language Journal* (2000), 74.

Sandstrom, N., J. Kaufman, and S. A. Huettel. "Males and Females Use Different Distal Cues in a Virtual Environment Navigation Task." *Brain Research: Cognitive Brain Research* (1998), 6: 351–360.

Saucier, D., et al. "Are Sex Differences in Navigation Caused by Sexually Dimorphic Strategies or by Differences in the Ability to Use the Strategies?" *Behavioral Neuroscience* (2002), 116: 403–410.

Silverman, I., and M. Eals. "Sex Differences in Spatial Abilities: Evolutionary Theory and Data." In J. Barkow, L. Cosmides, and J. Tooby (Eds.), *The Adapted Mind: Evolutionary Psychology and the Generation of Culture* (487–503). New York: Oxford University Press, 1992.

GRAY AND WHITE MATTER PROCESSING DIFFERENCES

Cordero, M. E., C. Valenzuela, R. Torres, and A. Rodriguez. "Sexual Dimorphism in Number and Proportion of Neurons in the Human Median Raphe Nucleus." *Developmental Brain Research* (2000), 124: 43–52.

Diamond, M. "Male and Female Brains." Lecture for Women's Forum West Annual Meeting, San Francisco, CA, 2003.

Gur, R. C., et al. "Sex Differences Found in Proportions of Gray and White Matter in the Brain: Links to Differences in Cognitive Performance Seen." Study: University of Pennsylvania Medical Center, May 18, 1999. [www.sciencedaily.com/releases/1999/05/990518072823.htm]

Gur, R. C., et al. "Sex Differences in Brain Gray and White Matter in Healthy Young Adults." *Journal of Neuroscience* (1999), 19.

STRUCTURES IN THE BRAIN

De Lacoste, M., R. Holloway, and D. Woodward. "Sex Differences in the Fetal Human Corpus Callosum." *Human Neurobiology* (1986), 5 (2): 93–96.

Hamann, S., et al. "Men and Women Differ in Amygdala Response to Visual Sexual Stimuli." *Nature Neuroscience* (2004), 4.

Jessel and Moir, *Brain Sex*, 1992.

Joseph, R., Ph.D. *Neuropsychiatry, Neuropsychology, and Clinical Neuroscience*, 3rd ed. New York: Academic Press, 2000.

Killgore, W. D., M. Oki, and D. A. Yurgelun-Todd. "Sex-Specific Developmental Changes in Amygdala Responses to Affective Faces." *NeuroReport* (2001), 12: 427–433.

Killgore, W. D., and D. A. Yurgelun-Todd. "Sex-Related Developmental Differences in the Lateralized Activation of the Prefrontal Cortex and Amygdala During Perception of Facial Effect." *Perceptual and Motor Skills Journal* (2004), 99.

Kilpatrick, L.A., D. H. Zald, J. V. Pardo, and L. F. Cahill. "Sex-Related Differences in Amygdala Functional Connectivity During Resting Conditions." *NeuroImage* (1 April 2006), 30 (2): 452–461. [http://today.uci.edu/news/release_detail.asp?key=1458]

Kimura, D. *Sex and Cognition*. Cambridge, MA: MIT Press, 1999.

Schlaepfer, T. E., G. J. Harris, A. Y. Tien, L. Peng, L. Seog, and G. D. Pearlson. "Structural Differences in the Cerebral Cortex of Healthy Female and Male Subjects: A Magnetic Resonance Imaging Study." *Psychiatry Research: Neuroimaging* (29 September 1995), 61 (3): 129–135.

Shors, T. J. "Significant Life Events and the Shape of Memories to Come: A Hypothesis." *Neurobiology of Learning and Memory* (2006), 85: 103–115. [www.rci .rutgers.edu/~shors/pdf/Significant%20life%20events%202006%20Shors%20article .pdf]

BRAIN CHEMISTRY: OUR NEUROCHEMICALS AND HORMONES

Albers, H. E., K. L. Huhman, and R. L. Meisel. "Hormonal Basis of Social Conflict and Communication." In D. W. Pfaff, A. P. Arnold, A. M. Etgen, S. E. Fahrbach, and R. T. Rubin (Eds.), *Hormones, Brain, and Behavior*, Vol. 1 (393–433). New York: Academic Press, 2002.

Christiansen, K. "Behavioral Effects of Androgen in Men and Women." *Journal of Endocrinology* (2001), 170 (1).

Compaan, J. C., et al. "Vasopressin and the Individual Differentiation in Aggression in Male House Mice." *Annals of the New York Academy of Sciences* (June 1992), 652: 458.

Liu, L. "Keep Testosterone in Balance: The Positive and Negative Effects of the Male Hormone." *WebMD*, January 2005.

DID YOU KNOW? MEN AND WOMEN REACT
TO STRESS DIFFERENTLY

Arletti, R., A. Benelli, and A. Bertolini. "Oxytocin Involvement in Male and Female Sexual Behavior." *Annals of the New York Academy of Sciences* (1992), 652 (1): 180–193.

John Hunkin, conversation with Barbara Annis, 2004.

Shors, T. J. "Stress and Sex Effects on Associative Learning: For Better or for Worse." *The Neuroscientist* (2001), 4: 353–364.

Shors, T. J., and G. Miesegaes. "Testosterone in Utero and at Birth Dictates How Stressful Experience Will Affect Learning in Adulthood." *Proceedings of the National Academy of Sciences* (15 October 2002), 99: 13955–13960.

Weiss, L. A., M. Abney, E. H. Cook, and C. Ober. "Sex-Specific Genetic Architecture of Whole Blood Serotonin Levels." *American Journal of Human Genetics* (2005), 76: 33–41.

Wood, G., and T. J. Shors. "Stress Facilitates Classical Conditioning in Males, but Impairs Classical Conditioning in Females Through Activational Effects of Ovarian Hormones." *Proceedings of the National Academy of Sciences* (1998), 95: 4066–4071.

DID YOU KNOW? MALE BANTER IS A
SECRET OF MALE POWER

Biddulph, S. "Real Male Friends." Chapter 9 in *Manhood: A Book About Setting Men Free.* Sydney: Finch Publishing, 1994.

Braden, W. R. *Homies: Peer Mentoring Among African-American Males.* LEPS Press, 1999.

Clawson, M. A. *Constructing Brotherhood: Class, Gender, and Fraternalism.* Princeton, NJ: Princeton University Press, 1989.

Decapua, A., and D. Boxer. "Bragging, Boasting and Bravado: Male Banter in a Brokerage House." *Women and Language* (Spring 1999), 22 (1).

DID YOU KNOW? MEN HAVE A BIOCHEMICAL CYCLE TOO!

Cutler, W., M.D. *Love Cycles: The Science of Intimacy.* Athena Institute Press, 1996. (Orig. pub. 1991.)

Lichterman, G. "Men's Room: The Male Hormone Cycle." [www.myhormonology.com]

CHAPTER THREE

UNDERSTANDING HOW MEN AND WOMEN
LEAD DIFFERENTLY

For more on the effect of cingulate gyrus differences, see "The Gendered Brain." [http://scienceblogs.com/cortex/2007/09the_gendered_brain.php]

Jennifer Allyn, interview with David Creelman, 2007.

Management experts Sophie Hahn and Anne Litwin have written on gender differences in leadership as a chapter in *Managing in the Age of Change: Essential Skills to Manage Today's Workforce,* edited by Roger A. Ritvo, Anne Litwin, and Lee Butler (Burr Ridge, IL: Irwin Professional Publishing, 1995). They provide a very useful graph in that chapter of observed differences. Many of their observations and ours are in sync, though they come from a more sociological perspective and we come from a more sociobiological one. Parallel research of this kind, even including slight differences, is very useful in corroborating gender differences for leaders.

TRANSFORMING YOUR TEAM

The two comments from media reports are modified for narrative flow and anonymity from the following sources: Marmol, G. G., and R. M. Murray Jr. "Leading from the Front." *McKinsey Quarterly* (1995), 3. [www.mckinseyquarterly.com/article_page.asp x?ar=104&L2=39&L3=29&srid=190&gp=0]; Muoio, A. "Women and Men, Work and Power." *Fast Company,* February 1998, 13: 71.

Also of interest in this area are the following:

- Alimo-Metcalfe, B. "An Investigation of Female and Male Constructs of Leadership and Empowerment." *Women in Management Review* (1995), 10 (2): 3–8.
- Alimo-Metcalfe, B., and J. Alban-Metcalfe. *The Transformational Leadership Questionnaire (TLQ).* Leeds: LRDL.

• "The Bottom Line: Connecting Corporate Performance and Gender Diversity." Catalyst, 2004.
• "Fiorina Comments on Public Firing." *CBS News, 60 Minutes*, 8 October 2006. [www.cbsnews.com/stories/2006/10/05/60minutes/main2069703_page3.shtml]
• Rosener, J. "Ways Women Lead." *Harvard Business Review*, November/December 1990, 119–125.
• Sharpe, R. "As Leaders, Women Rule." *BusinessWeek Online*, 20 November 2000.
• "Special Report: Women of Tech." *BusinessWeek Online*, 29 May 2003.
• "Women Effective Leaders for Today's World." *Northwestern News*, 4 August 2003. [www.northwestern.edu/univ-relations/media_relations/releases/2003_08/leadership.html]

PART TWO

THE TOOLS: PUTTING GENDER INTELLIGENCE TO WORK IMMEDIATELY

Note: A number of the brain facts we taught in Part One are applied and used more fully in Part Two. We do not carry those references forward in the four chapters of Part Two, but instead provide you with (1) a number of further clinical studies that have particularly informed our development of these GenderTools, and (2) further clinical studies that corroborate those we noted under Part One. Should you enjoy scientific reading, you may very much enjoy delving into these additional resources:

• Achiron, R., S. Lipitz, and A. Achiron. "Sex-Related Differences in the Development of the Human Fetal Corpus Callosum: In Utero Ultrasonographic Study." *Prenatal Diagnosis* (2001), 116–120.
• Allen, L. S., and R. A. Gorski. "Sexual Dimorphism of the Anterior Commissure and Massa Intermedia of the Human Brain." *Journal of Comparative Neurology* (1991), 312: 97–104.
• Anokhin, A. P., et al. "Complexity of Electrocortical Dynamics in Children: Developmental Aspects." *Developmental Psychobiology* (2000), 36: 9–22.
• Belsky, J. "Quantity Counts." *Developmental and Behavioral Pediatrics* (June 2002), 167–170.
• Blanton, R. E., et al. "Gender Differences in the Left Inferior Frontal Gyrus in Normal Children." *NeuroImage* (2004), 22.
• Blum, D. *Sex on the Brain: The Biological Differences Between Men and Women.* New York: Penguin Books, 1998.

CHAPTER FOUR

GENDERTOOL I: IMPROVING YOUR NEGOTIATION SKILLS WITH BOTH GENDERS

Candice Fuhrman, interview with Michael Gurian, 2007.

Darlene Mann and Sharon Patrick are quoted from *Women and Men, Work and Power*, by Anne Mouio, Fastcompany.com, January 1998 [www.fastcompany.com/magazine/13/womenofpr.html]

CHAPTER SIX

GENDERTOOL 3: IMPROVING YOUR COMMUNICATION SKILLS WITH WOMEN AND MEN

Jennifer Allyn, interview with David Creelman, 2007.

FOCUSING ON VERBAL COMMUNICATION

Bremner, J. D., et al. "Gender Differences in Cognitive and Neural Correlates in Remembrance of Emotional Words." *Pscyhopharmacology Bulletin* (2001), 35.

Phillips, M., M. Lowe, J. T. Lurito, M. Dzemidzic, and V. Matthews. "Temporal Lobe Activation Demonstrates Sex-Based Differences During Passive Listening." *Radiology* (2001), 220: 202–207.

Salomone, R. *Same, Different, Equal.* New Haven, CT: Yale University Press, 2003.

Schmidt, R. "Understanding Male and Female Brain Differences: The Adult Brain." *Family Therapy Magazine* (July/August 2004), 3 (4).

Schneider, F., U. Habel, et al. "Gender Differences in Regional Cerebral Activity During Sadness." *Human Brain Mapping* (2000), 9: 226–238.

Shaywitz, B. A., S. E. Shaywitz, et al. "Sex Differences in the Functional Organization of the Brain for Language." *Nature*, 16 February 1995, 373: 607–609.

Sowell, E., et al. "Development of Cortical and Subcortical Brain Structures in Childhood and Adolescence: A Structural Magnetic Resonance Imaging Study." *Developmental Medicine and Child Neurology* (2002), 44: 4–16.

Sowell, E., A. Toga, et al. "Mapping Cortical Change Across the Human Life Span." *Nature Neuroscience* (2003), 6 (3): 309–315.

FOCUSING ON NONVERBAL COMMUNICATION

Hall, J. A. *Nonverbal Sex Differences: Communication Accuracy and Expressive Style.* Baltimore: Johns Hopkins University Press, 1984.

Hall, J. A., and D. Matsumoto. "Gender Differences in Judgments of Multiple Emotions from Facial Expressions." *Emotion* (2004), 4.

Hall, J. A., J. D. Carter, and T. G. Horgan. "Status Roles and Recall of Nonverbal Cues." *Journal of Nonverbal Behavior* (2001), 25: 79–100.

Horgan, T. G. "Thinking More Versus Less About Interpreting Nonverbal Behavior: A Gender Difference in Decoding Style." Unpublished doctoral dissertation, Northeastern University, 2001.

Marano, H. E. "The Opposite Sex: The New Sex Scorecard." *Psychology Today* (July/August 2003), 38–44.

McClure, E. B., et al. "A Developmental Examination of Gender Differences in Brain Engagement During Evaluation of Threat." *Biological Psychiatry* (2004), 55.

McGivern, R. F., K. L. Mutter, J. Anderson, G. Wideman, M. Bodnar, and P. J. Huston. "Gender Differences in Incidental Learning and Visual Recognition Memory: Support for a Sex Difference in Unconscious Environmental Awareness." *Personality and Individual Differences* (1998), 25: 223–232.

McGuinness, D., and Symonds, J. "Sex Differences in Choice Behavior: The Object-Person Dimension." *Perception* (1977), 6: 691–694.

McKelvie, S. J. "Sex Differences in Memory for Faces." *Journal of Psychology* (1981), 107: 109–125.

McKelvie, S. J., L. Standing, D. St. Jean, and J. Law. "Gender Differences in Recognition Memory for Faces and Cars: Evidence for the Interest Hypothesis." *Bulletin of the Psychonomic Society* (1993), 31: 447–448.

Nowicki, S., Jr., and M. P. Duke. "Nonverbal Receptivity: The Diagnostic Analysis of Nonverbal Accuracy (DANVA)." In J. A. Hall and F. J. Bernieri (Eds.), *Interpersonal Sensitivity: Theory and Measurement* (183–198). Mahwah, NJ: Lawrence Erlbaum, 2001.

Powers, P. A., J. L. Andriks, and E. F. Loftus. "Eyewitness Accounts of Females and Males." *Journal of Applied Psychology* (1979), 64: 339–347.

Seidlitz, L., and E. Diener. "Sex Differences in the Recall of Affective Experiences." *Journal of Personality and Social Psychology* (1998), 74: 262–271.

Shapiro, P. N., and S. Penrod. "Meta-Analysis of Facial Identification Studies." *Psychological Bulletin* (1986), 100: 139–156.

Thayer, J. F., and B. H. Johnsen. "Sex Differences in Judgment of Facial Affect: A Multivariate Analysis of Recognition Errors." *Scandinavian Journal of Psychology* (2000), 41.

For many more science-based studies on male/female differences in reading and remembering verbal and nonverbal cues, go to the end of this Notes and Resources section. We've included a bonus section of fascinating studies.

TRY THIS: SELLING TO MEN

Our thanks to Karen Purves for sharing her wisdom with us. Learn more about her work at www.innovativeimpact.com.

CHAPTER EIGHT
HELPING WOMEN: RETAINING, MOTIVATING, AND WORKING WITH FEMALE TALENT

Mary Beth Backoff, interview with David Creelman, 2007.

Maria Ferris, interview with Barbara Annis, 2007.

Sean McConkey, interview with David Creelman, 2007.

Yezdi Pavri, interview with David Creelman, 2007.

"Study: Women Buy More Tech Than Men." *CNN.com*, 16 January 2004.

Wegert, T. "Marketing to Women: More Than a Media Buy." *ClickZ.com*, 18 May 2006.

SUCCESS STORIES: HOW GENDER-BALANCED LEADERSHIP IMPROVES THE BOTTOM LINE

All Catalyst studies are available through www.catalystwomen.org.

See also: Tahmincioglu, E. "When Women Rise." *Workforce Management*, September 2004. [www.workforce.com/section/06/feature/23/83/13/index.html] This article includes positive financial results at Ernst & Young. For positive results at GE, see also: Sellers, P., and J. Mero. "Power: Do Women Really Want It? That's the Surprising Question More of Them Are Asking When They Ponder Top Jobs in Business, Academia, and Government." *CNN.com*, 13 October 2003. [http://money.cnn.com/magazines/fortune/fortune_archive/2003/10/13/350932/index.htm]

INNOVATIONS IN THE TECHNOLOGY SECTOR: FEATURING IBM

Ted Childs, conversation with Barbara Annis, 2005.

Maria Ferris, conversation with Barbara Annis, 2007.

Harvard Business Review, 82, 9, "IBM Finds Profit in Diversity," David A. Thomas, September 27, 2004.

INNOVATIONS IN THE FINANCIAL SECTOR: FEATURING DELOITTE & TOUCHE

Yezdi Pavri, conversation with Barbara Annis, 2007.

Babcock, L., and S. Laschever. *Women Don't Ask*, NY: Bantam, 2007.

WHAT WOMEN WANT? NO, WHAT WOMEN NEED!

Carey, S. "More Women Take Flight in Airline Operations." *Wall Street Journal*, 14 August 2007.

Also of interest: Kageyama, U. "Women Climb Nissan Ladder." Associated Press, 16 July 2007.

John Maxwell, interview with David Creelman, 2007.

OBSTACLE 3: "WOMEN DON'T CARE, SO WHY SHOULD WE?"

Hewlett, *Off-Ramps, On-Ramps*, 2007.

OBSTACLE 6: GOOD OLD BOY NETWORKS

Maria Ferris, conversation with Barbara Annis, 2007.

Sharon Roberts, conversation with Michael Gurian, 2006.

Sharon Roberts is the author of a number of very useful articles, including "Selling to Women," which can be accessed through her website, www.R2ASSOC.com.

OBSTACLE 7: "WE DON'T HAVE A PROBLEM"

Mary Beth Backof, interview with David Creelman, 2007.

The Gallup survey can be found in *Now, Discover Your Strengths*, by M. Buckingham and D. O. Clifton. New York: Free Press, 2001. Studies and articles of related interest include the following:

Armour, S. "More Nursing Moms Get Lactation Programs at Work." *USA Today*, 15 May 2005.

Catalyst Group. "The Double-Bind Dilemma for Women in Leadership." 17 July 2007.

Choi, C. "Some Firms Give Moms a Real Break." Associated Press, 19 August 2007.

Chong, J.-R. "Study Says Men Prefer Blue, Women Like Lavender." *Los Angeles Times*, 21 August 2007.

Conant, E. "Trying to Opt Back In." *Newsweek*, 28 May 2007.

Hymowitz, C. "A Different Track." *Wall Street Journal*, 16 April 2007.

St. George, D. "Majority of Working Moms Prefer Part Time." *Washington Post*, 12 July 2007.

"The Journal Report: How to Fill the Talent Gap." *Wall Street Journal*, 15–16 September 2007.

Websites that may be of interest:

- www.WomenandBiz.com
- www.thewildwe.com
- www.womenbizowners.org
- www.ewomennetwork.com
- www.damselsinsuccess.com
- www.mompreneursonline.com

CHAPTER NINE

HELPING MEN: RECOGNIZING MEN'S LEADERSHIP STRENGTHS AND SOLVING ISSUES MEN FACE

COMPETITIVE SYSTEMS THINKING AND SYSTEMS PROTECTION

Baron-Cohen, *The Essential Difference*, 2003.

Maria Ferris, conversation with Barbara Annis, 2007.

"The 'Masculine' and 'Feminine' Sides of Leadership and Culture: Perception vs. Reality." Knowledge@Wharton, 5 October 2005. [http://knowledge.wharton.upenn.edu/article.cfm?articleid=1287]

Taylor, S. E. *The Tending Instinct*. New York: Times Books/Holt, 2002.

Van Honk, J., and D.J.L.G. Schutter. "Testosterone Reduces Conscious Detection of Signals Serving Social Correction." *Psychological Science* (2007), 18: 8.

Van Vugt, M., D. De Cremer, and D. P. Janssen. "Gender Differences in Cooperation and Competition." *Psychological Science* (2007), 18: 1.

DID YOU KNOW? MEN AND WOMEN CARE ABOUT INDIVIDUALS DIFFERENTLY

Blakemore, J.E.O., S. R. Baumgardner, and A. H. Keniston. "Male and Female Nurturing: Perceptions of Style and Competence." *Sex Roles: A Journal of Research* (April 1988), 18 (7–8): 449–459.

Grant, I., and M. Grant. "What Women Wished Men Knew About Them." *Parenting*, Autumn 2007, 68.

Taylor, *The Tending Instinct*, 2002.

MEN NEED WORK/LIFE BALANCE

Braiker, B. "Just Don't Call Me Mr. Mom." *Newsweek*, 8 October 2007, 53.

"Daddy's Brains." *Parent*, January 2006. The Princeton study discovered that connections in the male prefrontal cortex (executive decision making) increased, as did male bonding chemicals.

Gray, P. B., et al. "Marriage and Fatherhood Associated with Lower Levels of Testosterone." *Evolution and Human Behavior* (2002), 23.

Harman, W. S., et al., "The Psychology of Voluntary Employee Turnover." *Current Directions in Psychological Science* (2007), 16: 1.

CHAPTER TEN

GENDERTOOL 5: PRACTICING GENDER-INTELLIGENT MENTORING AND COACHING IN YOUR CORPORATION

Ensher, E., and S. Murphy. *Power Mentoring*. San Francisco: Jossey-Bass, 2005. Of further interest:

- Allen, T. D., and L. T. Eby. "Factors Related to Mentor Reports of Mentoring Functions Provided: Gender and Relational Characteristics." *Sex Roles: A Journal of Research*, January 2004.
- Ding, W. W., F. Murray, and T. E. Stuart. "Gender Differences in Patenting in the Academic Life Sciences." *Science Magazine*, 3 August 2006. [www.kauffman.org/items.cfm?itemID=727]
- "First Findings Reported in Survey on Faculty Careers." *News from Harvard Medical, Dental & Public Health Schools*, 24 October 2003. [http://focus.hms.harvard.edu/2003/Oct24_2003/advancement.html]
- Mikko, C., and S. Gilbert, Eds. "Women at Work." *UMN News*, 4 January 2005. [http://www1.umn.edu/umnnews/Feature_Stories/Women_at_work.html]
- Morris, A. "Leaving Your Mentor, the Right Way." *Wall Street Journal*, 3 April 2007.
- Sharpe, R. "As Leaders, Women Rule." *BusinessWeek Online*, 20 November 2000.
- Tahmincioglu, E. "When Women Rise." *Workforce Management*, September 2004. [www.workforce.com/section/06/feature/23/83/13/index.html]
- Tharenou, P. "Does Mentor Support Increase Women's Career Advancement More Than Men's? The Differential Effects of Career and Psychosocial Support." *Australian Journal of Management* (June 2005), 30 (1).
- Wadhwa, V. "Fixing Engineering's Gender Gap." *BusinessWeek Online*, 14 March 2006. [www.businessweek.com/smallbiz/content/mar2006/sb20060314_760860.htm]

THE IMPORTANCE OF MENTORING AND COACHING IN GENDER SCIENCE

Brady, D., and J. McGregor. "What Works in Women's Networks." *Business Week*, 18 June 2007.

Fisher, H. *Anatomy of Love*. Random House, Inc., 2000.

"Women's Way of Mentoring." August 1998. [fastcompany.com]

Zachary, L. J. *The Mentor's Guide*. San Francisco: Jossey-Bass, 2000.

FURTHER RESEARCH ON GENDER, MEMORY, CLOTHING, AND BODY IMAGE

Three particular areas of clinical brain/gender research that can be fascinating for workplace and corporate teams are memory, clothing, and body image/sensory differences.

Memory Differences

Casiere, D. A., and N. L. Ashton. "Eyewitness Accuracy and Gender." *Perceptual and Motor Skills* (1996), 83: 914.

Davis, P. J. "Gender Differences in Autobiographical Memory for Childhood Emotional Experiences." *Journal of Personality and Social Psychology* (1999), 76: 498-510.

Doherty, R. W. "The Emotional Contagion Scale: A Measure of Individual Differences." *Journal of Nonverbal Behavior* (1997), 21: 131-154.

Herlitz, A., L. G. Nilsson, and L. Backman. "Gender Differences in Episodic Memory." *Memory and Cognition* (1997), 25: 801-811.

Herrmann, D. J., M. Crawford, and M. Holdsworth. "Gender Linked Differences in Everyday Memory Performance." *British Journal of Psychology* (1992), 83: 221-231.

Horgan, T. G., et al. "Gender Differences in Memory for the Appearance of Others." *Personality and Social Psychology Bulletin* (2004), 30 (2): 185-196.

Gender and Clothing

Buckley, H. M., and M. E. Roach. "Clothing as a Nonverbal Communicator of Social and Political Attitudes." *Home Economics Research Journal* (1974), 3: 94-102.

Davis, L. L. "Clothing and Human Behavior: A Review." *Home Economics Research Journal* (1984), 12: 325-339.

Douty, H. "Influence of Clothing on Perception of Persons." *Journal of Home Economics* (1963), 55: 197-202.

Feinberg, R. A., L. Mataro, and W. J. Burroughs. "Clothing and Social Identity." *Clothing and Textiles Research Journal* (1992), 11: 18-23.

Johnson, B. H., R. H. Nagasawa, and K. Peters. "Clothing Style Differences: Their Effect on the Impression of Sociability." *Home Economics Research Journal* (1977), 6: 58-63.

Kaiser, S. *The Social Psychology of Clothing*. New York: Macmillan, 1990.

Knapp, M. L., and J. A. Hall, *Nonverbal Communication in Human Interaction*. Belmont, CA: Thomson Learning, 2002.

Kwon, Y. "Sex, Sex-Role, Facial Attractiveness, Social Self-Esteem and Interest in Clothing." *Perceptual and Motor Skills* (1997), 84: 899-907.

Lundberg, J. K., and E. P. Sheehan. "The Effects of Glasses and Weight on Perceptions of Attractiveness and Intelligence." *Journal of Social Behavior and Personality* (1994), 9: 753–760.

Mathes, E. W., and S. B. Kempher. "Clothing as a Nonverbal Communicator of Sexual Attitudes and Behavior." *Perceptual and Motor Skills* (1976), 43: 495–498.

Sporer, S. L. "Clothing as a Contextual Cue in Facial Recognition." *German Journal of Psychology* (1993), 17: 183–199.

Gender and Body Image

Cross, S. E., and L. Madson. "Models of the Self: Self-Construals and Gender." *Psychological Bulletin* (1997), 122: 5–37.

Driscoll, D. M., J. R. Kelly, and W. L. Henderson. "Can Perceivers Identify Likelihood to Sexually Harass?" *Sex Roles* (1998), 38: 557–588.

Gabriel, S., and W. L. Gardner. "Are There 'His' and 'Hers' Types of Interdependence? The Implications of Gender Differences in Collective Versus Relational Interdependence for Affect, Behavior, and Cognition." *Journal of Personality and Social Psychology* (1999), 77: 642–655.

Harris, M. B., R. J. Harris, and S. Bochner. "Fat, Four-Eyed, and Female: Stereotypes of Obesity, Glasses, and Gender." *Journal of Applied Social Psychology* (1982), 12: 503–516.

Jackson, L. A., L. A. Sullivan, and J. S. Hymes. "Gender, Gender Role, and Physical Appearance." *Journal of Psychology* (1987), 121: 51–56.

Jobson, S., and J. S. Watson. "Sex and Age Differences in Choice Behavior: The Object-Person Dimension." *Perception* (1984), 13: 719–724.

APPENDIX: GENDER/BRAIN SPECTRUM SURVEYS FOR MEN AND WOMEN

These are useful tools for helping you identify where your particular male or female brain might fit on the gender spectrum. These tools can lead to interesting insights, "Aha!" moments, and discussion, though they are not the final word on who you are!

The survey for men appears first, then the survey for women. You'll notice that a lot of the language repeats, as the tools are set up as mirror images of one another. An earlier version of the survey for men appeared in Michael's book *What Could He Be Thinking?*

Gender/Brain Spectrum Survey for Men

On a blank sheet of paper, list A, B, and C. For each of the following scenarios, pick only one answer, the one that is closest to how you would react. The questions are phrased as if you are married, but you can expand them to fit your life situation. Give each A answer 3 points, each B answer 2 points, and each C answer 1 point.

1. When you and your wife are discussing a social gathering you have both attended, and she says, "Did you notice Tim and Sarah seem to be having marital issues?"
   A. Tim and Sarah's relationship isn't something you want to talk about.

   B. Now that you think about it, there might be something to what your wife is saying, but at the party you didn't really notice anything.

   C. You noticed trouble between Tim and Sarah right away.

2. When you and your wife channel-surf in front of the television, how important is possession of the remote control to your enjoyment of the de-stressing and bonding time together?

   A. You often become irritated if you don't control it, as she will want to watch programs that bore or agitate you.

   B. You do need to have control for enjoyment, but you're okay with her having control some of the time.

   C. You don't really care which channels she goes to and what you watch during the de-stressing and bonding time.

3. When you and your wife talk about things that happened years or decades ago, she remembers how the room looked, what people said, colors of walls, other sensory and verbal details.

   A. You never or rarely remember these sorts of incidents with as much detail.

   B. You often remember them with as much detail.

   C. You have as good a memory as your wife does for sensory and verbal details.

4. Your wife complains that you don't listen to her, and this has created frustration during your marriage.

   A. A lot of the time.

   B. Some of the time.

   C. Never or almost never.

5. When focused on your computer or completing some other concentrated task, you become mildly agitated, impatient, or irritable at being interrupted by your wife (or another person) to talk or answer questions unrelated to your present task.

   A. A lot of the time.

   B. Some of the time.

   C. Rarely.

6. When your wife has had a difficult day, is quite stressed, is hurting regarding her relationship with you or another person, and wants to talk all of it out with you:
   A. You feel anxious.
   B. You listen for a short time, then suggest solutions.
   C. You feel great about the opportunity to connect with her feelings and explore them with her verbally.

7. When you see a group of children or young people playing street hockey or basketball or some other physical game and a boy falls down:
   A. You quickly say something like, "No bones broken, you're fine. Get up and get back in there!"
   B. You wait a few minutes to see what he will do, and if he doesn't get back in the game, you encourage him to do so.
   C. You physically move over to him and help him feel better.

8. When you "retire" and have lots of free time, you want to:
   A. Exercise as much as your body can take, play a physical game that involves a little bit of competition, work on a project or hobby that allows you to build or repair something.
   B. Relax, read a book, watch the sunset, call a friend and chat.
   C. Shop, preferably with someone else who loves this task as you do.

9. When you are driving alone, or when you go on a family trip or outing, it is important for you to know where north/south and east/west are, and other points on a map:
   A. More than it is for your wife.
   B. About the same.
   C. Less than it is for your wife.

10. While you and your wife are sitting together reading books or written material for work, the radio or stereo is on in the background, and changes from one song to another.
    A. You are less likely than she is to comment on the song change.
    B. You and she note the change of song and comment on it similarly.

    C. You are more likely than she is to note the song change and even comment on it.

When you have completed the survey, total your points. The highest possible score is thirty; the lowest is ten. Wherever you land on this spectrum is normal, and this isn't the final word, of course—the survey is meant to be an entertaining way of getting to know yourself and other men a little better. As you score your survey, you may get a glimpse of where you fit on the spectrum, from the extreme male brain all the way to bridge brain.

If you score between twenty and thirty, you may be more toward the farther male side of the spectrum. If you score below twenty, you may lean more toward the middle. Of course, to really know where you fit, you'd have to undergo a number of brain scans. For now, we hope that this book, this survey, and the BBC online survey ("What Sex Is Your Brain?" www.bbc.co.uk/science/humanbody/sex/add_user.shtml) can be helpful, without the expense of a scan.

Gender/Brain Spectrum Survey for Women

On a blank sheet of paper, list A, B, and C. For each of the following scenarios, pick only one answer, the one that is closest to how you would react. The questions are phrased as if you are married, but you can expand them to fit your life situation. Give each A answer 3 points, each B answer 2 points, and each C answer 1 point.

    1. When you and your husband are discussing a social gathering you have both attended, who is most likely to say, "Did you notice Tim and Sarah seem to be having marital issues?"
       A. You noticed trouble between Tim and Sarah right away and brought it up first.
       B. Now that you think about it, there was trouble between Tim and Sarah, though you didn't notice right away.
       C. You don't want to discuss the trouble between Tim and Sarah because it's not really your business.

2. When you and your husband channel-surf in front of the television, how important is possession of the remote control to your enjoyment of the de-stressing and bonding time together?
   A. It's not important.
   B. It's somewhat important.
   C. It's very important.

3. When you and your husband talk about things that happened years or decades ago, who remembers how the room looked, what people said, colors of walls, other sensory and verbal details?
   A. You are generally, if not always, the one.
   B. You are often the one.
   C. He is more likely to be the one.

4. Your husband complains that you don't give him enough space, verbally and relationally, and this has created frustration during your marriage.
   A. A lot of the time.
   B. Some of the time.
   C. Never or almost never.

5. When focused on your computer or completing some other concentrated task, you become mildly agitated, impatient, or irritable at being interrupted by your husband (or another person) to talk or answer questions unrelated to your present task.
   A. Rarely.
   B. Some of the time.
   C. A lot of the time.

6. When your husband has had a difficult day, is quite stressed, is hurting regarding his relationship with you or another person, you want to move immediately to talking about it:
   A. A lot of the time.
   B. Some of the time.
   C. Rarely.

7. When you see a group of children or young people playing street hockey or basketball or some other physical game and a boy falls down:
   A. You quickly move over to the fallen boy to see if he's okay and help him up.
   B. You wait a few minutes to see what he will do, and if he doesn't get up, you encourage him to do so.
   C. You quickly say something like, "No bones broken, you're fine. Get up and get back in there!"

8. When you "retire" and have lots of free time, you want to:
   A. Shop and do other sensual tasks, preferably with someone else who loves these tasks as you do.
   B. Relax, read a book, watch a sunset, call a friend and chat.
   C. Exercise as much as your body can take, play a physical game that involves a little bit of competition, work on a project or hobby that allows you to build or repair something.

9. When you yourself are driving alone, or when you go on a family trip or outing, how important is it for you to know where north/south and east/west are, and other points on a map?
   A. Not very important; you guide yourself by using milestones, not maps.
   B. Somewhat important.
   C. Very important.

10. While you and your husband are sitting together reading books or written material for work, the radio or stereo is on in the background, and changes from one song to another.
    A. You are more likely than he is to comment on the song change.
    B. You and he note the change of song and comment on it similarly.
    C. You are less likely than he is to note the song change and even comment on it.

When you have completed the survey, total your points. The highest possible score is thirty, the lowest is ten. Wherever you land on this spectrum is normal, and this isn't the final word, of course—the survey is meant to be an entertaining way of getting to know yourself and other women a little better. As you score your survey, you may get a glimpse of where you fit on the spectrum, from the extreme female brain all the way to bridge brain.

If you score between twenty and thirty, you may be more toward the farther female side of the spectrum. If you score below twenty, you may lean more toward the middle. Of course, to really know where you fit, you'd have to undergo a number of brain scans. For now, we hope that this book, this survey, and the BBC survey ("What Sex Is Your Brain?" www.bbc.co.uk/science/humanbody/sex/add_user.shtml) can be helpful, without the expense of a scan.

THE AUTHORS

Michael Gurian is a corporate consultant, family therapist, and a *New York Times* best-selling author of twenty-five books, including eight national bestsellers, published in twenty-one languages. His brain-based trainings on gender and leadership, including *Leading Partners*, have been used around the world.

The Gurian Institute, which Michael cofounded in 1996, conducts research in gender diversity, provides consulting, and launches pilot programs. Michael has provided training at Cisco Systems, Boeing, Brooks Sports, and others, and consulted for government agencies in the United States and abroad, including the Washington State Department of Ecology and the U.S. Department of Justice.

Michael's work and the work of the Gurian Institute have progressed at the leading edge of gender relationships for twenty years, with seventy associates worldwide. Michael and his team believe that the future of male-female relationships depends on brain-based gender training becoming well used in corporations, communities, schools, and families.

Before becoming a consultant and lecturer, Michael taught at Gonzaga University, offering that university's first gender biology course. He has provided keynotes at Harvard University, Johns Hopkins, Stanford University, Macalester College, University of Colorado, University of Missouri, UCLA, and many others.

His work has been featured in *Time, Newsweek, People, Business Week,* the *Wall Street Journal, USA Today,* the *New York Times,* the *Washington Post,* the *London Times,* and other major print media, as well as on the *Today Show, Good Morning America, The View,* PBS, NPR, Bloomberg, MSNBC, and CNN.

Barbara Annis is a thought-leader, corporate keynoter, and CEO of Barbara Annis and Associates. With over twenty years as a specialist in gender issues in the workplace, Barbara's consulting firm has grown from a one-person team to an organization of twenty-seven associates now headquartered in New York, with offices in Tokyo, Sydney, and London. Barbara's client list includes IBM, Xerox, PricewaterhouseCoopers, Deloitte & Touche, HSBC, Nissan, and Goldman Sachs. Twenty companies she has worked with—most recently, Nissan Corporation—have won Catalyst Women and Diversity awards.

Barbara has designed and delivered programs on authentic leadership for women at Harvard University, where she serves on the Women's Leadership Board.

She is also the author of *Same Words, Different Language,* available in twenty countries worldwide.

To Bring Our Gender Training Programs to Your Corporation

This book is based on decades of training module development. As you can see from the book, the information and methodology of these programs can have a beneficial effect on a corporation's competitive edge, economic capital, and human resource development. Leadership teams that use the gender intelligence training programs discover exciting new ways to lead authentically, and experience financial advantage.

The training itself uses keynoters, personal coaches and trainers, as well as training workbooks, manuals, DVDs, Microsoft PowerPoint presentations, and interactive web tools. We are able to provide train-the-trainer models for your corporations, which can be sustained internally for years to come.

To bring gender intelligence training to your corporation, or just for more information about what we do, please visit www.gendertrainings.com.

INDEX